P R A Y E R S

O F   A

Y O U N G

P O E T

R E V I S E D   E D I T I O N

rainer maria rilke

translated and introduced by
mark s. burrows

PARACLETE PRESS
BREWSTER, MASSACHUSETTS

2016   First Printing This Edition

2013   First and Second Printing Hardcover Edition

Prayers of a Young Poet – Revised Edition

ISBN 978-1-61261-641-4

Library of Congress Cataloging-in-Publication Data

Names: Rilke, Rainer Maria. | Burrows, Mark S., 1955- translator.
Title: Prayers of a young poet / Rainer Maria Rilke ; translated and
   introduced by Mark S. Burrows.
Description: Revised edition. | Brewster, Massachusetts : Paraclete Press,
   2016. | Includes bibliographical references.
Identifiers: LCCN 2015038078 | ISBN 9781612616414
Subjects: LCSH: Prayer–Poetry.
Classification: LCC PT2635.I65 A2 2016 | DDC 831/.912–dc23
LC record available at http://lccn.loc.gov/2015038078

10 9 8 7 6 5 4 3 2 1

Published by Paraclete Press
Brewster, Massachusetts
www.paracletepress.com
Printed in the United States of America

FOR
MY FAMILY AND FRIENDS,
IN GRATITUDE FOR THEIR ABIDING.

"Jetzt heilt es leise unter uns."

RAINER MARIA RILKE

Contents

Preface

Works of art . . . cannot be reached through criticism. Only love can grasp them and go on to hold and interpret them aright. Trust yourself and your own judgments in this. . . . Give them over to their quiet, undisturbed way of evolving, which as with every sort of progress must arise from your inner depths and cannot be pressured or hurried in any way. Everything in this has to do with patient endurance until the time comes to give birth. Letting every impression and every seed of a feeling reach completion in its own way—in the dark, in the unsayable and unconscious, in experiences unreachable by reason alone—and, with deep humility and patience, awaiting the hour when a new clarity might come forth: this alone is what it means to live artistically, in understanding as in creating. . . . I learn daily and through suffering, for which I am grateful, that patience is everything.

RAINER MARIA RILKE,
LETTERS TO A YOUNG POET[1]

MORE THAN A CENTURY has passed since Rainer Maria Rilke (1875–1926) wrote these poems, yet they continue to draw readers as if they had first appeared only recently. This has much to do with their lyric beauty and with the way they startle us into new ways of seeing. It also points to the spiritual vitality that courses through them, and how they suggest what it might mean to "live artistically," as Rilke put it in a letter to a young poet named Franz Kappus. They do so by reaching toward what the poet describes as "the hour when a new clarity" might be birthed, drawing on the wellspring of tradition as voiced by a spiritual seeker whose yearnings offer guidance in an unsettled time.

These poems show us what it might mean to open more fully to the inner impulses of our lives, to make ourselves vulnerable to the outer world of the senses in order to let "every impression and every seed of a feeling" find its way in the deep place of soul within. But this takes patience. There are no short-cuts, no easy solutions or ready-made answers. And such discoveries, as Rilke suggests, while "unreachable through reason alone," do lie within the reach of our experience. As a whole, this collection—written in a burst of creativity during the last weeks of September and early October, 1899—explores the soul's journey in ways that are often startling and yet also strangely alluring, reflecting his devotion to a wisdom untamed by religious conventions and responsive to the deeper truths of life.

How are we to find our way into such depths? Rilke would have been puzzled by the question, knowing that the way itself is a journey of love by which we learn to give our lives, as with works of art, "room"—the word belongs to the poet's core vocabulary—to grow, without narrowing our expectations to our preconceptions or the demands of what is familiar. In this sense, the poems stand in the long tradition of literature we find within yet also beyond the boundaries of religious communities, writings we have come to call "mystical." Rilke may not be a mystic, properly speaking (though this question continues to be vigorously debated), but these poems surely belong to the genre in its broadest and truest sense. This ought to remind us that to understand them, as with all art, vulnerability trumps mastery, and "patience is everything."

On the surface, Rilke crafts these poems as the prayers of an old orthodox monk and icon painter who, in the opening poem, invites us to overhear him as he speaks of his vocation:

> The hour bows down and stirs me
> with a clear and ringing stroke;
> my senses tremble. I feel that I can—
> and seize the forming day.

Already we sense that the poet's gift has to do with the kind of attention he brings to life, an offering he sees as the seeds of his art given to meet the longings of others. Everything matters for this to transpire in the patience of waiting, the openness of heart, and the fullness of devoting oneself to what is *real*, in both the material and spiritual realms within and beyond us. In the process, we find ourselves called to bear witness to the whole of life in the particulars, to what we are aware of as well as what lies hidden "in the dark, in the unconveyable, the unconscious" of our experience. As he goes on to put it in this initial poem:

> Nothing is too small for me, and I love it anyway
> and paint it on the golden base and large—
> and hold it high; and I don't yet know *whose*
> soul this might yet free. . . . [1]

He thus views the artist's life not as a sacrifice but as an offering, a way of opening, to and through the yearnings we share with others. This is one reason these poems, as with Rilke's work generally, draw us as they do.

The poems of this collection call us to look both outward and within, to seek the divine in the ordinary details of both everyday life and in the mystery of our inner life. Rilke dares to address God with the intimate "You," though never in a clichéd manner. He confesses, too, that, while "a thousand theologians plunged / into the ancient night of Your name" [55] and "the poets scattered You about" as if "a storm passed through their stammering," [56] he intends to approach God differently, boldly claiming that

> I don't want to know where You are;
> speak to me from every place. [52]

All of the poems in this volume chronicle this search for the divine in the sanctuary of the soul, though he persistently reminds us that this yearning is to find its proper shape in how we experience *ourselves* and our *world*. For Rilke, "inner" and "outer" are but dimensions of the larger whole of spiritual experience, often carrying us beyond the familiarities of creed and doctrine. Originality is not his aim, but authenticity surely is.

————

Rilke published these poems, six years after first writing them, as the opening section of *The Book of Hours* titled "The Book of Monkish Life" (1905). In the original version from which this translation has been made the narrative voice of an old orthodox monk and icon painter sounds with a particular clarity—in part because of the "notes" Rilke first added to many of the poems (here printed in italics). Yet this literary conceit does not limit their appeal, perhaps because the monk's courage in embracing life no matter what comes—whether darkness or light, despair or delight—is one we readily grasp as our own. We hear him call out to us confidently in one of the poems late in this sequence:

I know, whenever my thinking takes stock:
how deep, how long, how wide—
You are and are and are,
having trembled all about in time. [64]

But he also tells of his struggle at the heart of this quest, for this God whom he at times experiences as a "neighbor," close by, is more often a severely felt absence. "You dwell far off in Your outermost house," he laments, but in the same breath goes on to insist that "Your whole heaven listens within me." [18] This apparent distance ultimately leads Rilke to affirm the role of receptivity and openness over competence and certainty.

This sense of longing—ours for God and God's for and even *in* us—lends an intimate voice to these poems, one shaped by an expectancy that leads the poet to address God with a daring claim: "If You're the dreamer, I'm Your dream." [19] Indeed, he goes on in a later poem to suggest as if in a reminder that "You are the beginning, God, and I, Your servant, am for You a new start." [21]

These poems as prayers have found their way into the hearts of many late-modern readers because of their distinctive blend of lyric vitality and spiritual authenticity. Included in this collection are poems that number among the most celebrated and cherished of Rilke's writings. Perhaps this is because, as prayers, they pulse with that rare blend of daring and humility we seek in spiritual literature, knowing how it can move us in the depths of our heart. As these poems voice their song within us, they invite our yearning for authentic spirituality amidst the external pressures and inner anxieties we experience. The story these prayers tell—on the surface, that of an old monk's journey through seasons of difficulty and delight, in struggle and praise—never seems far from our own. As they unfold, we discover with the poet that it is precisely the "dark hours" of our lives that open us to new horizons, inviting us to find "that [we] have room for a second life, timeless and wide." [5] We sense with Rilke that the spiritual life has less to do with finding answers than it does with "living the questions."[2]

But here, a warning: those for whom the spiritual life is about learning to "intone loud names" for God, who have "forgotten already about [God's] nearness," [66] will make little sense of these prayers. They may even seem threatening. But if you desire spiritual authenticity without sacrificing intellectual honesty, they might encourage you with Rilke to "believe in everything that has not yet been said." [12] For these are poems that invite us into a soulful journey, calling us to live with the audacious hope of a seeker who "feels the radiance of a new page / on which everything could still come to be," [8] as Rilke puts it. Their allure lies in the strength of this invitation, in the rare blend of beauty and wisdom that shapes them, and in their posture of confidence and humility, When taken and read as prayers in this sense, they invite us to see life as a "ripening" and accept its movements as an "expansive return," as a flow that carries us "into the broad arms of the open sea." [12]

———

Finally, and as a guide to the reading of these poems, two notes are in order: first, the italicization and punctuation found in these poems reflect Rilke's at times idiosyncratic usage; and, second, the brief notes often found after—and, in rare cases, before—the poems are Rilke's own, added by the poet as if they were entries written to chronicle the monk's experience. At his publisher's request, he did not include these in what became the later published version in *The Book of Hours*, primarily as a matter of stylistic consistency, because the second and third sections of this later publication ("The Book of Pilgrimage" and "The Book of Poverty and Death") lacked such notes. This is in ways an understandable editorial decision, but a regrettable artistic omission, because in many cases these brief descriptive comments deepen our understanding of the poems individually and as a whole. And, in the case of the final poem in the collection, the note—which is a poem in its own right—points to a crucial level of meaning unrecognizable by a bare reading of the poem alone. Here, the "you" addressed by the old monk is no longer God, but rather the last of the "Kobzars," the wandering bards of the Ukraine whose work it was to maintain the tradition of song among the people. This poem, as the finale of the cycle, thus reads as an engaging invitation to the reader: ours is the task not to look for this old bard, but rather to give voice to these songs for the sake of our own life and that of the community. And here, as Rilke had reminded the young poet Mr. Kappus, patience is of utmost importance, and neither criticism nor memory but finally love alone is what keeps art—and our very souls—alive. This is the experience of "the Open" that shapes these poems and might reshape our lives.

Mark S. Burrows
Bochum, Germany

THE PRAYERS

[1]

The hour bows down and stirs me
with a clear and ringing stroke;
my senses tremble. I feel that I can—
and seize the forming day.

Nothing was yet done before I beheld it,
and every becoming stood still;
my ways of seeing are ripe, and, like a bride,
to each one comes the thing each wills.

Nothing is too small for me, and I love it anyway
and paint it on the golden base and large—
and hold it high; and I don't know *whose*
soul this might yet free . . .

On the 20ᵗʰ of September in the evening after a lengthy rainstorm,
when the sun suddenly broke through the forest's dark canopy and
through me.[3]

[2]

I live my life in widening rings
which spread out to cover everything.
I may not complete the last one,
but I'll surely try:

I'm circling around God, around the ancient tower,
and I've been circling for thousands of years—
and I don't yet know: am I a falcon, a storm,
or a vast song. . . .

On the same evening, as again wind and clouds appeared.

[3]

Many of my robed brothers in cloisters
to the south dwell beneath the shade of bay trees.
I see how their Madonnas look so utterly human,
and dream of Titan's paintings,
how God glows in them like embers.

But when I settle into my own soul I know
my God is dark and like a clump
of a hundred roots drinking silently.
I lift myself from *His* warmth;
more than this I don't know, for my branches
rest in the depths and sway gently in the winds.

On the same evening, in the study.

[4]

We dare not paint You in our own pose,
You dawning one from whom the morning rose.
We take from our old palettes
the same strokes and the same beams
with which the holy one held You silently.

We build paintings before You like walls
so that thousands of them now surround You—
for our pious hands veil You whenever
our hearts simply open to behold You.

On the same evening.

[5]

I love the dark hours of my being,
for they deepen my senses;
in them as in old letters I find
my daily life already lived
in holy words, so soft and subdued.

From them I've come to know that I have room
for a second life, timeless and wide.

And at times I'm like the tree, ripe and rustling,
standing above the dead boy's grave,
gathering him in its warm roots,
fulfilling the dream he'd lost
in sorrows and songs.

In the woods, on the 22nd of September.

[6]

You, neighbor God, when I sometimes
wake You with loud knocks in the long nights,
I do so because I rarely hear You breathing
and know You're alone in the vast hall.
And when You need something, no one's there
to offer a drink to Your outstretched hand.
I'm always listening. Give me a little sign;
I'm very near.

Only a thin wall lies between us—
by chance; for it could be
that a cry from Your mouth or from mine—
and down it would fall
without any noise or sound at all.

This wall stands tall with Your icons.

And they stand before You like names.
And when the light flames in me
and claims You in my deep,
it wastes itself as radiance upon their frames.

And my senses, which darken so soon,
are without a home and parted from You.

[7]

If only it could all for once be so utterly still . . .
if the accidental and approximate
were muted, including the neighbor's laugh,
and if the noise my senses keep making
didn't hinder me in waking,
then I could think You in a thousand-fold
thought all the way to Your bounds,
and own You—if only in the moment of a smile—
and thus give You as a gift to everything alive
like a word of thanks.

*Upon returning home through the forest in the evening, a storm arose
and the treetops fell silent in the midst of it, listening breathlessly:*

[8]

I'm living just as the century departs.
One feels the wind from a large leaf
that God and you and I had written on,
which turns above by hands no one knows.

One feels the radiance of a new page
on which everything could still come to be.

Tranquil powers measure its breadth,
regarding each other with dark intent.

*As the monk returned home, a bright and flaming blush rose into the
heavy grey of the western sky, convincing the clouds to take on a new
and unusual violet hue. An evening unlike any that had ever been
waited behind the trembling trees, and he discerned this at the cen-
tury's turning as a sign and bowed before it. 22nd of September, 1899.*

[9]

I read it out from Your word,
from the story of the gestures
You made with Your hands for what is becoming,
having brought them bounding round, wise and warm.
You said "living" aloud, and whispered "dying,"
and repeated "being" again and again.
But murder came before the first death,
a rip running right through Your ripened circles,
and a casket emerged,
tearing voices apart
that had gathered
to utter You
and bear You,
a golden bridge . . .

And what they stammered about since
are fragments
of Your old name . . .

As the monk read the Bible one storm-swept evening, he found that the murder of Abel occurred before death first entered the world. This terrified him in the depths of his heart.

[10]

Gripped with fear, he went out into the dark forest, opening himself to all the light and to all the fragrances and to the many pious sounds of the forest that sang louder than the confused stammering of his thoughts. And a dream came to him on a night soon thereafter that he rendered with these lines:

The pale young Abel speaks:
I am no more. My brother did something to me
that my eyes didn't see.
He hid the light
from me.
He pushed my face
away
with his.
He is now alone
and must surely always remain so;
because no one does to him what he did to me—
all walked on my path,
all must face his anger,
all are lost in him;
for I believe that my brother keeps watch
like a tribunal;
the night took thought of me,
not of him.

The 22ⁿᵈ of September, late.

[11]

And then the monk gave thanks with a liberated heart:

You, darkness from which I come,
I love you more than the flame
that bounds the world,
shining
in a single ring
beyond which no creature knows of it.

But the darkness seizes everything,
folds and flames—
how it grasps them,
people and powers . . .

And it is possible that a great strength
stirs near where I dwell.

I believe in nights.

Also on the 22nd.

[12]

I believe in everything that has not yet been said.
I want to free my most pious feelings;
what no one has ever dared to want
will suddenly become my nature.

If this is impudent, my God, forgive me.
But with this I want to tell You
that my noblest power should be an instinct,
and thus without anger and without hesitation—
this is how children cherish You.

With this flood, with this flow
into the broad arms of the open sea,
with this expansive return,
I want to bear witness to You; I want to proclaim You
like none before.

And if this is pride, then let me be proud
in my prayer,
which stands so earnest and alone
before Your shadowed brow.

The same night.

[13]

I am too alone in this world, and yet not alone enough
to consecrate every hour;
I am too small in this world, and yet not little enough
to be present before You like a thing,
dark and clever.
I want my will, and want to attend to my willing
all the way to my doing;
and what I want, in such calm and somehow hesitant times—
when something draws near—
is to be among the wise,
or else alone.

I want to mirror You always in full form,
and never want to be blind or too old
to hold Your heavy, wavering image.
I want to show myself:
nowhere do I want to be stooped in stature,
because that would be for me a lie.
And I want my perception
to hold true before You. I want to describe myself
like a painting I once gazed upon,
long and near—
like a word I understood,
like a poem I polished,
like my daily tankard,
like my mother's face,
like a ship
that carried me safely
through the deadliest storm . . .

[14]

You see that I want much;
perhaps I want everything:
the dark held in each unending demise
and the light-trembling game in every rise.

So many live who want nothing,
ennobling themselves through the fleeting feelings
of their own judgment.

But You delight in every face
that serves and thirsts.

And you delight in all who use You
like a tool.

You aren't yet cold, and it's not too late
to plunge into Your forming depths
where life quietly reveals itself.

[15]

We build on You with trembling hands
and construct towers, atom upon atom.
But who could ever complete You,
You cathedral?

What is Rome?
It is crumbling.
What is the world?
It will be shattered
before Your towers are topped with domes,
before Your beaming brow rises
from the miles of mosaic tiles.

But sometimes in a dream
I'm able to survey
Your room—
deep from its beginning
to the rooftop's golden ridge.

And I see: my senses
shape and build
the last adornments.

The 22ⁿᵈ of September.

[16]

Because someone once desired You,
I know that we, too, may desire You.
Even if we renounce all depths:
when gold lies deep in the mountains
and no one's there to dig for it,
one day the river brings it to the surface,
reaching in stillness into the stones,
into their fullness.

Even when we don't desire:
God ripens.

[17]

He who reconciles the many paradoxes of his life
and grasps them gratefully in a symbol
drives
the noisy crowd from the palace
and celebrates differently, and You're the guest
he receives on soft evenings.

You're the second in his solitude,
the quiet center of his soliloquies,
and every ring drawn around You
spans for him the circle out of time.

The 22nd, in the night.

[18]

Why do my hands go astray with the brushes?
Whenever I *paint* You, God, You scarcely notice.

I *feel* You. You begin to tremble
on the hem of my senses as with many islands—
and to Your eyes that never blink
I am the room.

You no longer dwell in the midst of Your radiance
where all the ranks of the angel-dances,
the farthest ones, fade away from You like music,—
You dwell far off in Your outermost house;
Your whole heaven listens within me,
for in my pondering I didn't speak myself to You.

*The monk had many strange thoughts, and they lingered with him
like a crowd of guests; then he turned back to God and wrote these
fervent lines.*

*The 24th of September, written in the forest among the people who'd
gone out for Sunday walks.*

[19]

I am! You anxious One, don't You hear me
with my soft senses surging toward You?
My feelings, which have found wings,
circle around Your face innocently.
Don't You see my soul standing right
in front of You in a cloak made of stillness?
Doesn't my May-like prayer ripen
in Your sight like fruit upon a tree?

If You're the dreamer, I'm Your dream.
But if You want to wake, then I'll be Your will
and partake of all Your splendor
and round myself like a stillness among the stars
above the strange city of time.

*The monk becomes buoyant in his depths and feels himself gifted in all
things and present in every joy, like the radiance that recognizes itself
in all the gold of this world. And he climbs up above his poetry, as if
atop a flight of stairs, and no longer grows weary from it.*

[20]

My life is not this steep hour
in which You see me hurrying so.
I am a tree standing before what I once was;
I am only one of my many mouths,
and, at that, the first to close.

I am the stillness between two notes
that don't easily harmonize,
because the note Death wants to lift itself up . . .

But in the dark interval both come,
trembling, to join as one. . .
                    and the song sings on, beautiful.

After this, the monk drew very near to God; on the same evening.

[21]

And for beauty's sake we're both
consecrated wondrously to a *single* work.
We're like images deeply stained in old silk.
And whether I paint or dream or suffer,
I hang like a sparkling necklace
around the darkness of Your shoulders.

Beauty's the meaning of all being.
Initially she took from hidden loins
the false folds of a shabby gown;
raw joy was tamed before her,
and because of her, yearning and grief
wear slender dazzling crowns.

She'll change values that have grown heavy;
for she alone is entirely just.
You're the beginning, God, and I, Your servant,
am for You a new start . . .

She will give us this: to be without end.

*The monk had almost become an artist, though he allowed himself to
be shaped by his poems rather than shaping them.*

[22]

And the monk folded his hands and stood in the middle of a moonlit
night like the trees standing near him in pious and humble darkness.
And thus he mastered his many feelings so that they became poems,
though they leaped into words from chaos and wildness.

If I'd grown up in some place
graced with easier days and simple hours,
I'd have made for You a great celebration,
and my hands wouldn't have held You
the way they sometimes do in clutching fear.

There I'd have dared to squander You,
You unbounded present!

Like a ball
I'd have thrown You high in all my surging joys
so that someone could catch You,
springing to meet You
with ready hands in the arc of Your fall,
You, thing of all things.

I'd have let You flash
like a sword!
From the most golden orbit
I seized Your fire,
and it held it for me
above the whitest hand.

I'd have painted You: not on the wall
of heaven itself, from edge to edge;
I'd have formed You like a giant
would form You: as mountain, as fire,
as wind gathering from desert sand—

or:
it could be that I'd found
You once . . .
    My friends are so far away
that I hardly hear their laughter ringing—
and You, You who've fallen from the nest,
are a young bird with yellow talons
and large eyes, and make me sad—
my hand is much too broad to hold You;
with my finger I lift a drop from the well
and listen to tell if You'll take it in your thirst;
and I feel Your heart and mine pounding—
and both from fear.

[23]

The last part of this poem occurred to the monk as he came running
breathlessly from the monastery garden, crossing the threshold to enter
his small, dimly lit cell. By then the poem was already complete. It
brought such harmony and mirth to him that he quickly prepared for
bed and determined to sleep that night without further pondering or
prayer. And just before falling asleep, this little poem came to him,
and he recognized it with a smile:

I find You in all the things
I'm at ease with and like a brother;
as seeds You warm Yourself in the least of things,
and give Yourself to the great ones in their ripening.

This is the wondrous play of powers
that passes obediently through things:
growing in the roots, vanishing in the trunks,
and rising in the treetops like a resurrection.

The 24ᵗʰ, late.

[24]

But in this night the monk was woken by one of his brothers whom he heard crying in a nearby cell. When he recognized the sound in his wakened ears, he arose, put his belt on over his robe, and went to his brother. Immediately the younger monk grew silent. The awakened one carried his brother—his face moist with tears, his demeanor silent and antagonistic. Into the pale beam of moonlight streaming through the window, he took a clasped book, opened it at random and commenced to read from the gleaming pages:

I pass away, I pass away,
like sand running through fingers of the hand.
And suddenly I have so many senses,
all in their different ways thirsting.
I feel myself swelling and aching
in a hundred places,
above all in the depths of my heart.

I want to die. Leave me alone.
I'll surely be
so racked with fear
that my pulse will burst within me.

[25]

Then the monk rejoiced:

Look, God, here comes another who wants to build on You,
one who yesterday was but a child, his hands still folded
in prayer as women taught him to do,
a gesture that already half lies.

For the right hand wants to free itself from the left,
to defend itself or wave about
alone at arm's end.
Still yesterday his brow was like a stone
in the stream, rounded by the days
that mean nothing more than a pounding of waves
and demand nothing else than to carry an image
of heaven that chance drapes over it;
today a history of the world
urges itself
upon some unrelenting court of law,
and then sinks beneath the weight of its verdict.

Room will come upon a new face.
There was no light before this light . . .

And, as never before, Your book begins.

24ᵗʰ, in the night.

[26]

I love You, You softest law
by which we ripened in our wrestling;
You, great homesickness we'd not mastered;
You, forest from which we never emerged;
You, song we sang in every silence;
You, dark net
within which our fleeing feelings were snared.

You'd begun Yourself with such unending vastness
on that day when You began with us—
and we were so ripened in Your suns,
had become so wide, so deeply planted,
that now in resting You can complete Yourself
in humans and angels and icons of the Madonna.

Let Your hand rest on the ledge of heaven
and mutely endure what we darkly do to You.

On a day when there seemed no end to the rain, mushrooms stood up in the forest with their strangely large heads all around the tree trunks, and there was hardly enough light shining upon this world to see the radiance playing upon the wet leaves of the blood-red, withering vine.

On the 26th, toward evening.

[27]

Workers we are: apprentices, journeymen, masters,
and we build You, You lofty nave;
now and then an earnest traveler comes,
passing like radiance through our hundred minds,
showing us with trembling hands some new hold.

We climb into the swaying scaffolding,
in our hands the hammer hanging heavily,
until the hour came that kissed us on the brow,
one beaming from You as if it knew everything,
drifting like the wind across the wild sea.

Then comes a clanging of many hammers,
the mountains quaking from the proud blow;
only when it grows dark do we let You go:
and Your coming contours begin to dawn . . .

God, You are vast.

On the 26ᵗʰ, again toward evening.

[28]

You're so vast that nothing's left of me
when I stand anywhere near You.
You're so dark that my little brightness
makes no sense along your seam.
Your will flows like a wave
and every day drowns within it.

Only my yearning reaches up to Your chin
and stands before You like the greatest of angels—
one who's unknown, pale and yet unredeemed,
who holds out to You the reach of his wings.

He no longer wants that shoreless flight
by which the paling moons swam by,
knowing by now enough of worlds.
He wants to stand with his wings,
as with flames, before Your shadowed face,
wants to see in their glistening shine
if Your gray brows will damn him.

The monk trembled before the next poem as if it came in answer to this one; the 26th.

[29]

So many angels came searching for You in the light,
thrusting their brows toward the stars in the height,
wanting to know You in all that is bright;
but whenever I write of You, I find that they
distance themselves with faces turned aside
from the folds of Your robe,

for You were only a guest of this gold.
Only to oblige that age when they
entreated You with their clear and marbled prayers
did You reveal Yourself as the King of comets,
proud of the rays that streamed across Your brow.

You turned homeward when that time melted away.

Utterly dark is Your mouth from which I drifted astray,
and Your hands are of ebony.

In remembrance and anticipation.

[30]

I'd read about the life
of Michelangelo in foreign books.
As an artist he faced proportions
gigantic in size,
and forgot about immeasurability.

He always returns to dwell among us
in times when the yearning for a sense of completion
leads us to seek values that are true.
Then someone raises the great weight of the age
and heaves it into the abyss of his breast.

Those who came before him knew pleasure and pain,
but he still feels the great mass of life
and grasps it all as if it were but *one* thing.
God alone remains beyond the reach of his will;
still he loves Him, though with a great disdain
for His unattainability.

*The monk knew of Michelangelo's "Moses" from a picture he'd seen
in a large book, and became acquainted with his unfinished "Pietà"
from a drawing.*

[31]

The branch from God the tree that reached across all Italy
has already bloomed.
It might have liked
to hasten becoming heavy-laden with fruit,
but grew weary at the height of its blossoming—
and now will yield no more.
It felt only the spring of God's presence,
and only His Son, the Word,
came to fruition.
All strength turned
toward this beaming boy.
All came bearing offerings
for Him;
all of them, like cherubim,
sang His praises.
And He gave off a soft fragrance
as the Rose of all roses,
and was a circle
surrounding the homeless,
wandering in disguises and changes
among all the rising voices of time.

The 26th, on the same evening.

[32]

Then the mother was loved as well,
because there, in her girlhood's will
that held her, astonished and still—
such wondrous paths appeared.

Then a blossoming came upon her,
and her sacred story
manifested itself anew, and in a new light:
not a wooden cottage made of spruce,
but marble columns like verse,
and wind and sun upon the face,
and a place: golden and green.

Only now and then did she think upon the troubles
that wrapped her soul in gloom,
and crept forth out of the wide and precious frames
in the evenings when only a few supplicants came
like poor debtors—
and bowed to the saddest of painters—
and whispered . . .

On the 26th.

[33]

That's the way she was painted—above all by the one
who bore his yearning directly from the sun.
She ripened for him more purely in riddles,
but in suffering became more and more like us:
throughout his entire life he was like a mourner
whose weeping pounded tears into his hands.

He is the most exquisite veil for the pains
that clung to her bruised lips,
and at times he bent them nearly into a smile—
not even by the light of seven angel-candles
will his secret be won.

*The monk came to see that in his paintings Mary has already set out
upon her way. Centuries before she'd gone forth from the silvered icons
to wander through the world, taking various forms and in manifold
deeds. When she grows tired, she'll return to her place in the icons and
lay her child again in the silver cradle, sitting with him there and
singing to him . . . For the times are like a circle, and that day is fes-
tive indeed when something ripe falls into the beginning that's always
waiting to start.*

On the 26th, in the evening.

[34]

With a branch which was never like that one,
God the tree will eventually come, announcing
summer and murmuring with ripeness.
In a land where people lean closer to hear,
where everyone is just as lonely as I.

For this will be revealed only to the solitary,
and even more will be given to many others
who share this solitude than to the poor one.
For to each a *different* God appears
until they recognize, close to tears,
that through their wide-open pondering,
through all their knowing and negating,
differing only among His hundreds,
one God wanders like a wave.

This is the most definitive prayer
that those keeping watch declare:
God the root has borne fruit;
go forth and shatter the bells.
We come to the quieter days
in which the hour stands ripe;
God the root has borne fruit:
be earnest and watch.

This was revealed to the monk in his most pious night.

The 26ᵗʰ, in the night.

[35]

I can't believe that the little death
we glimpse day by day over our shoulder
should remain a worry that afflicts us.

I can't believe that death is seriously a threat.
I'm still alive and have time to create instead,
and longer than the roses my blood stays red.

My sense is deeper than the clever game
with our fear that death so delights in.
I am the world
from which in its straying death fell.

—

                              Like death,
the circling monks wander about,
and we fear their return,
never knowing—is it always the same one?
Are there two, are there ten, are there a thousand or more?
We know only this strange yellow
hand
that reaches out to us, so naked and near—
there, there:
as if it came forth from our own robe.

On the 26th.

[36]

What will You do God when I die?
I am Your tankard—when I shatter?
I am Your drink—when I go sour?
I am Your robe and Your calling;
when I'm gone You'll lose your meaning.

After me You'll have no house where
soft and warm words might greet You,
and the satin sandals which I am
will fall from Your weary feet.

Your vast cloak releases You,
and Your gaze that I now receive,
as with a duvet which warms my cheek,
will come and search for me—persistently—
and lay itself with the setting sun
into the lap of stones unknown.

What will You do God? I'm afraid . . .

That night the monk chose to call death to his mind more often than before; and with regard to so many things, he considered death the enemy he and God shared in common.

On the 26th, in the night.

[37]

🎋

In the morning, when the monk woke from a deep sleep, he spoke earnestly to the sun:

You're the murmuring embers
sleeping on all the ovens, far and wide.
For knowing happens only in time,
but You're the dark unconscious one:
from eternity to eternity.

You're the one pleading and afraid
who burdens the sense of all things;
You're the syllable heard in the song,
trembling ever more and returning
under duress in voices that are strong.

You never taught Yourself differently:

For You're not the one keenly sought
around which wealth orders its ways;
You're the simple one who saves,
You're the peasant with the beard:
from eternity to eternity.

Blessed with this poem, the monk greeted the day; the 27th of September, a morning marked by sun and storm.

[38]

*In turbulent nights, the monk thought again about the young brother
he'd recently found weeping, and spoke to him in the Spirit:*

You, yesterday a boy whom chaos came to:
don't squander your blood in blind passion!
You aren't after enjoyment but rather joy.
You were raised to become a bridegroom,
and shame should rise to be your bride.

This great desire yearns also for you;
all arms are suddenly bare,
and in pious paintings pale cheeks
take on the heat of unfamiliar fires;
your senses are like many snakes
which, stained in red's varied shades,
stretch out to the tambourine's beat.

All at once you find yourself left utterly alone
with your hands that detest you—
what, then, if your will can't do a miracle . . .

But through it all rumors of God wander
in your dark blood as if along dark alleys.

[39]

Pray, then, as that one teaches you,
the one who returns from the chaos
and keeps his focus on the holy ones
who hold the dignity of their being,
painting their beauty as if with a sword,
in enameled gold upon the icons' board.
He teaches you to say:
                 You, my deeper sense,
trust that I won't disappoint You;
there's much clamoring in my blood—
but I know I'm made of yearning.

A great earnestness comes upon me,
and within its shadow life is cool.
For the first time I'm alone with You—
You, my feeling.
You're so like a maiden.

There was a woman in my neighborhood
who tempted me in her fading garments.

But You speak to me from such distant lands,
and my strength
looks up to the ridges of the eastern hills.

On the 29ᵗʰ of September, after fearful nights.

[40]

Because the monk had written these things, that very day an archan-
gel appeared to him dressed in a simple flowing gray robe. It was the
angel who'd been chosen for him from eternity, whose brow held the
fullness of a thousand days. And behind this apparition, a warm red
radiance lingered; surrounded with this, the monk began to write:

I have hymns that I hold silently;
there's an integrity deep in me
in which I bow my senses down.
You regard me as tall, but I'm small.
You distinguish me in the dark
from things that kneel;
they're like flocks grazing for a meal,
and I'm the shepherd on the sloping heath
who draws them home at dusk.
Then I come following behind them,
hearing in muffled shuffling the darkened bridges,
and in the smoke rising from their backs
my return is concealed.

The 29th, in the evening.

[41]

God, how do I grasp that hour of Yours
when You thrust Your voice ahead of You,
wandering as it does all around in the room?
For You, the void was like a wound—
and so You cooled it in creating the world.

Let the healing now come quietly among us.

For the past ages drank
many fevers from one who was convulsed with disease,
and already *we* feel in the swaying ease
the beat pulsing quietly behind.

We lie soothingly upon the void,
and cover over all that is torn.
But You grow into the uncertainty
that lies within the shadow of Your face.

*The monk considers the history of his own land, and feels the many
ways it covered over fevers. But he recognizes at the same time that
much in this history had become whole and calm.*

On the evening of the 29th.

[42]

The night was still wild, but the monk found the morning in this
good prayer:

All who busy their hands—
not in time, in the poor city,
all who lay them on what is quiet
in a place far from trodden paths
that hardly has a name anymore,
these give voice to You, You daily blessing,
and utter softly upon a page:
    Ultimately there are only prayers;
    our hands are consecrated for this,
    and have done nothing but implore;
    whether we've painted or hayed,
    in the daily labor with tools
    a kind of piety shows forth.
    For time has many forms;
    now and then we hear about it
    and do what is eternal and old,
    so that every hour unfolds
    as if the world were still young.
    We know God walled us all around
    like a beard and a robe.
    We are the veins of basalt
    in God's severe majesty.

30th of September, before the day's work had begun.

[43]

The name is for us like a light
placed upon our brow;
I cast my face down
before this seasoned judgment.
And I saw—and it speaks of this ever since—
You, great darkening weight
bearing down on me and on the world.

You pried me slowly loose from time
in which, though faltering, I climb,
and I bowed down after gently struggling:
now Your darkness comes lingering
in Your gentle victory.

Now You have me, but don't know *who,*
for Your senses that spread so far
see only that I had become dark.
You hold me very tenderly,
and listen as I stroke my hands
through Your old beard.

*The monk never thinks about the profane name he had in the world.
But the name he now bears as a monk seldom suits him; it's only a
bridge across which the archangel's words travel to sing an "Ave"
within his soul.*

[44]

Your very first word was: *light.*
Then time came forth. After that You kept a long silence.
Your second word was *man,* and fear entered in—
we still darken at the sound of it—
and again Your face grows pensive.

I don't want Your third.
I often pray in the night: Be the mute one
who continues to grow in the ways You appear,
whom the Spirit drives on in our dreams,
inscribing the steep cost of keeping silence
upon our brows and mountain ranges.

Be our refuge from the anger
that banished the unsayable.
Night fell in paradise:
Be the watchman with his horn
of whom one says only that he blew upon it.

On the 1ˢᵗ of October, a bright autumn Sunday when the monk's
yearning led him to wander back and forth along a long avenue lined
with withering linden trees.

[45]

In my cell there are often bright carnations—
like stars between roof beams, between thoughts—
and they gaze into my soul:
this is where I like to stand,
or in parks, fading and windless,
with evenings and ponds and avenues;
there You came to me most frequently.

There I recognized You most readily
whom I cannot always distinguish clearly;
there my love lifted You from the land,
and my whole being became silk,
surrounding us like a mantel
that concealed and joined us both.

From that place strength and stillness came to me.
When my senses bless me in this way,
then no one else can meet me
as I wander down nearby streets,
only You, You coming one—only You.

On the 1ˢᵗ of October, as the evening came to autumn and to our hands.

[46]

You come and go. Doors close
more softly now, almost without stirring.
You're the quietest of all those who
pass through these quiet houses.

We can become so used to You
that we don't look up from the book,
its pictures becoming so beautiful,
Your shadow draping them in blue—
because all things always intone You,
at times quietly, at times loud.

Often when I see You with my senses
Your vast form falls into fragments;
You walk with the lightness of deer
while I am dark and am forest.

You are a wheel on which I stand;
among Your many dark spokes
one overcomes the others continually,
and turning brings You closer to me—
my willing works expand
from one return to the next.

On the same day, as it grew darker.

[47]

You are the deepest one who towers,
the envy alike of divers and of spires.
You are the soft one who spoke forth,
and yet when a coward inquired of You,
You indulged Your reticence and fell quiet.

You are the forest of contradictions.
I could rock You like a child,
and yet Your curses reach their goal
and wreak havoc among the people.

The very first book was written for You,
and the first image tempted You;
You were present in suffering and in loving,
and Your earnestness was inscribed as if in bronze
on every face which sought likenesses of You
in what creation, with its seven days, brought forth.

You lost Yourself among thousands in the crowd,
and the proud sacrifices all grew cold
until You stirred Yourself in high church choirs
behind the golden doors,
and the fear that was born
girded You with form.

The 1ˢᵗ of October.

[48]

I know: You're the mysterious one
around whom time stood hesitantly still.
O how beautifully I shaped You
with my proud hand
in the hour that punished me so.

I sketched many elegant drafts,
faced all the hindrances—
until these plans fell apart;
the lines and rounded shapes
became tangled like thornbushes
until suddenly, deep within me
from a thrust into uncertainty,
the most pious of forms sprang forth.

I can't survey the breadth of my work,
yet I feel that it stands now complete.
But when I turn my eyes aside
I want to build it once again.

This, then, is the monk's piety, which estranges God only on the day
when he no longer struggles with Him anew.

1ˢᵗ of October.

[49]

This is my daily work over which
my shadow lies like a shell.
And even if I'm like leaves and loam,
whenever I pray or paint
it becomes Sunday once again, and in the valley
I'm the voice of a praising Jerusalem.

I'm the proud city of the LORD,
and speak of Him in a hundred tongues;
David's gratitude has resounded within me:
I lay in twilights of sounding harps
and in-breathed the evening star.

My paths lead to the East—
and if long ago the people forsook me,
they did it so that I might grow.
I hear each one pacing within me,
and widen my solitudes
from one new beginning to the next.

*The monk sang with a loud voice as evening fell such that all the
brothers opened their hearts, and instead of chanting their evening
prayers this great song passed among them like a king.*

The 1ˢᵗ of October.

[50]

You, the many cities not yet attacked,
open wide the gates of Topas.
Their lanes are muted by grass,
but within the smoothness of their walls
the day shows forth like gold and glass.

Once you've striven for a single day
and evening has climbed into the crenels—
to which you give yourselves quietly
with every sense, and heavier in your hands—
then night will come for you and begin,
one that, like the dancers' dream,
lives from struggle and from discipline.

You'll be silvered from games,
now like a sea, now like a mouth,
warmed with roses, rounded with lights,
made beautiful with singing forms that rise
before darkness and what lies behind.

You'll become brides kissed
by princely liberators from afar,
and one whom you must greet
stands assembled before your veils
like a tower made of amethyst.

[51]

The monk sang this hymn in heightened rapture of soul. The cities
of this poem speak of those brothers who weren't yet open to the East;
because of this, they were able to bring nothing to completion, neither
the day of their labor nor the knowing night, and not even that night
which begins after the first evening—that deep and marvelous bridal
night filled with spiritual images and fearful gestures into which
angels climb, bearing salvation with them like "princely liberators
from afar." After that night, images and gestures must no longer
stand with faces veiled in the presence of the God who completes
Himself before them in the days of their shame.

I come home from the soaring
in which I'd lost myself.
I was song, and God the rhyme
still rustles in my ear.
I'll become quiet and simple again
and my voice will be still,
my face bowed
for a better prayer.
To others I was like a wind,
and in my stirring I called out to them;
I was far off in the place where angels dwell,
high up where light dissolves into the void—
but God darkens in the deep.
The angels are the last gusts
blowing the branches of His treetop—
and the way they pass through His boughs

is for them like a dream.
Their trust in the light is stronger
than in God's black power:
Lucifer fled
into their neighborhood.
He is Prince in the Land of Light,
and his brow stands upright
against the void's great glare
so that with singed face
he begs for darknesses.
He's the bright god of time,
waking it with his loud cry,
and because he often screams
in pain and in it often laughs,
time trusts his sanctity
and clings to his power.
Time is like the fading edge
of a beech tree's leaf,
the shining raiment
that God cast aside
when He, always seeking the deep,
grew tired of flight,
hiding Himself from every coming year
until the roots of His hair
grew slowly through all things . . .

*Thus the monk regretted the exuberance by which he'd allowed himself
to be seduced.*

1ˢᵗ of October.

[52]

We grasp You only in what we do,
illuminate You only with our hands;
our every sense is but a guest here,
yearning to reach beyond the world.

Every sense is conceived;
one feels its elegant hem,
and knows someone spun it—
but heaven surrenders itself
because it cannot choose.

I don't want to know where You are;
speak to me from every place.
Your willing evangelist distorts
everything, and in his forgetting
neglects to look for the resonance.

But I'm always approaching You
with all my coming;
yet *who* am I and *who* are You
when neither of us understands the other?

The monk's night prayer on the 1ˢᵗ of October, late at night.

[53]

My life has the same garment and hair
that all the tsars have at death's hour.
For power estranged only my mouth,
while the empires I gather silently
exalt themselves in what lies behind me,
and my senses are steadfast like royalty.

For them, praying is a way to edify,
to build from everything so that dread
becomes beautiful and like a vastness—
and every act of genuflecting and trust
(done so that others won't notice)
is topped by many domes—gold
and blue and brightly colored.

For what are churches and cloisters
with all their ascending and rising—
other than harps, those sounding consolers
that pass through the hands of the half-redeemed
in the presence of kings and maidens . . .

*2nd of October, early in the morning in the forest, and among deer
wandering through groves of trees golden with the day's first light, like
sounds rising from the strumming of sun-soaked strings.*

[54]

In his cell, hunched over books in the day's first light, the monk wrote:

God commands me to write:
Let cruelty befall kings,
for this angel comes before love,
and without this arch I'd have
no bridge to cross over into time.

God commands me to paint:
Time for me is the deepest pain.
I thus placed in its bowl:
a woman awake, the mark of wounds,
precious death to compensate,
fearful reveling in the cities,
madness and kings.

God commands me to build:
I am *king* of time.
To *You*, though, I'm only a somber
witness to Your solitude;
I'm the eye crowned with the brow . . .

The postscript of the monk:
All this I behold over my shoulder
from eternity to eternity.

2nd of October, at day's beginning before any work.

[55]

A thousand theologians plunged
into the ancient night of Your name;
young maidens wakened to You,
and young men girded in silver
shimmered in You, You battle.

Among Your long colonnades
poets encountered each other,
becoming kings of sounds—
mild and deep and masterful.

You're the soft evening hour
that makes all poets alike;
You enter darkly into their mouths,
and with the sense of discovery
each surrounds You with rich array.

A hundred thousand harps lift You
like a swinging out of quietude,
and Your old winds cast
to all things and needs
the breath of Your majesty.

2nd of October, beneath soft evening clouds.

[56]

The poets scattered You about;
a storm passed through their stammering—
but I want to gather You once more
in the vessel that pleases You.

I wandered forth in a great wind
where You'd moved thousands of times,
and I bring with me everything I find:
like a cup, the blind one needed You,
and at times a large part
of Your mind resided in a child.

You see that I'm a seeker—

one who wanders behind his hands
keeping silence, like a shepherd;
one whom all glances disgrace
that turn to gaze on his work,
such scrutiny leading it astray—
one who dreams of completing You
and: of becoming completed himself.

2nd of October.

*The room darkened around the monk as evening fell. And it seemed
to be filled with many forms and voices, all of which shone with the
last light of day.*

[57]

Seldom does the sun shine within the great church.
The walls grow larger from the shaping forms and,
surrounded by patriarchs and virgins,
the golden Royal Doors urge
themselves open like unfurling wings.

At the end of its columns
the wall disappears behind the icons,
and gemstones dwelling in silent silver
rise up like a choir
falling back again into the crowns,
keeping silent more beautifully than before.

Above them, blue like nights
and with a pale face,
she hovers who gladdened You, the woman
who is keeper of the gate, the morning dew
who blossoms around you like a meadow
without ceasing.

The dome is full of Your Son,
binding the whole church as one:
don't You want to make use of Your throne
which with my gaze I behold? . . .

On the 2nd of October, as the monk remembered the prayers he once offered in the Church of the Dormition in Moscow.

[58]

I entered as a pilgrim
and felt You seven times
on my brow, You stone;
with lanterns, seven in number,
I surrounded Your dark being,
and entered into every painting
with two kisses or three,
as if at dusk in a valley.

I stood there where beggars stand,
those dark and haggard ones:
from their drifting up and down
I grasped You, You wind.
Among them I saw a peasant ancient in years
and bearded like Mary's father Joachim,
and from the way he darkened—
surrounded by many others like him—
I sensed You like never before, so tenderly
revealed and wordlessly
in them all, and in him.

You grant movement to time,
and yet never rest in it:
the peasant finds Your sense—
lifts it up and throws it down
and lifts it up again.

On the same evening.

[59]

And with a dark piety the monk uttered the day's night prayer.

2nd of October.

> I watched for You for a long while
> as if lingering above wells and along walls.
> And if others were to come and find me sleeping:
> God, don't let go of me with Your hands,
> for I am night from Your night.
>
> Even when I sleep I am awake.
> Sunk in the hems of Your senses,
> I hear Your dreams like winds
> and willing like the trees I speak
> to You many syllables and strange.
>
> My sleep is a granite roof
> held up above Your body,
> and like a wondrous creek
> that gushed out of the mountains,
> my feelings are crushed there a thousandfold.

[60]

God speaks to each one of us only before we're made,
then wanders with us silently out of the night;
but the words uttered before each begins,
the misty words, are these:

"Go, you who are sent out by your senses;
go out to the boundary of your yearning;
clothe me with a garment.

Grow like a fire behind things
so that their shadows, spreading all about,
cover me always and utterly.
Let everything happen to you: beauty and dread.
One must only go; no feeling is too remote.
Don't let yourself part with me.
Near is the land
you call life.

You'll recognize it
by its earnestness!

Give me your hand."

On the 4ᵗʰ of October; early, before beginning the hard work.

[61]

I was among the oldest monks, the painters and keepers of
    myths.
They wrote their stories quietly and drew runes of glory.
In my visions I see with winds and waters and woods,
murmuring on the borders of *Christendom*—
You land that is not to be cleared.
I want to recount You. I want to gaze upon You and describe
    You
not with the base of red or face of gold but with ink from
    the bark of old apple trees;
I can't bind You with pearls to the leaves,
and You would be blind to the most trembling image
my senses could find, surpassing it with Your simple being.
I want to name things in You, modest and unadorned;
I want to name the kings, the first ones and where they
    came from,
I want to narrate their deeds and days along the margins of
    my pages.
For You're the ground; to You the times are ever like
    summer,
and You view those near at hand no differently than those
    in the far distances,
and what if they knew to plant You deeper and cultivate You
    better:
You feel Yourself veiled from many such harvests
and don't hear the reapers' sickles as they walk over You.

4th of October, early in the morning.

[62]

You, darkening ground! Patiently You endure the walls;
perhaps You'll let the cities endure for another hour,
grant two more hours to the churches and lonely
      monasteries,
leave five more hours of beauty for all the redeemed,
and see yet seven hours for the peasants' daily work—
before You again become forest and water and growing
      wilderness
at the hour of ungraspable fear—
then You'll demand to take back Your uncompleted likeness
from all things.

Give me a little more time; I want to love things in ways no
      one has yet done
until all of them become worthy of You and wide.
I want only seven days, seven,
on which no one has yet written—
only seven pages of solitude.

The one You give this book to, which includes these pages,
will stay hunched over its pages—
unless You take him in Your hands
and write these things Yourself.

On the 4ᵗʰ of October, at midday.

[63]

On this day the monk wrote a letter to his superior:

Most worthy Father and Metropolitan!
I beseech you, first of all, to bless me so that my soul might
    truly see.
I'm a monk living in the monastery consecrated to the Holy
    Ones.
I hardly know what guided me
so that my words, Lord, might touch you.
It doesn't seem fitting to give my pen free reign,
and of course I know nothing about worldly affairs.
Even this time I've told myself: you've often conquered
your urges and refrained from writing this letter,
but today that doesn't help at all. I'm afraid,
and it seems to me that something within us might die
if we fail to speak. Thus, Lord, I beg your forgiveness and
ask you to accept this voice that rises from my depths.

My life on the whole is like my robe,
my soul is like my face,
the deeds of my day are consecrated
by a will that doesn't draw attention to itself.
But I still love things that are in the light,
playing with colors like an ensemble of violins,
showing themselves in time while keeping silent
about what is of value to their roots and what has weight.

I live a holy life. I don't call upon any court,
and my prayer with which I exalt myself
and which I sometimes speak and sometimes live
is: *"Make me simple*
that I might become ever more whole in You."
I don't mean by this some struggle or ascetic discipline,
not the dream of Saint Therese
whose sanctity the Occident extols.
I've chosen what is less distinguished.
I look out across the land; I listen, pray, read,
and sometimes paint an icon of St. Nicholas
or the holiest one in the Stoglav style—
more than this I can't manage. I hallow my monastery,
Father. I wish to please you.

But occasionally I looked at the books
of Westerners with stories and Madonnas
and meager pictures of their churches.
Of course I'm not learned enough to ascertain
from this the meaning or purpose of their yearning,
but before one whom they call godly—
one of the archangels bears his name—
it occurred to me that they enjoy God
like a festival, like a summer that flows by
just as all things do,
and at this I dropped the book
as if it were sinful—because *my* God is difficult . . .
There are no paintings which signify God
and yet gladden an age
with all the achievements of its *particular* time.
Paintings rather are like the tolling of church bells,

immutable in their festivity.
How might God, pulled along by the dance of days,
remain the refuge for the afflicted
when such destitute times forced Him
to take a form shaped by fear and moments of darkness?
Amid sumptuous hours adorned
with their noblest splendor, how should God remain
among those who were uncertain and troubled?
Whatever an age has of strength and beauty
should turn them toward the many things
that arise from God, and end before them;
if heaven presses itself from their hands,
then paint God darkly on the walls
and give to every saint a page.
This is the room for which time shapes itself
in all its shy and heartfelt modesty.
Time testifies to love's endurance,
while gratitude transforms itself
within the daily press of life.
Tell me, Father, what they attain
with their art and clever science—
nothing of this is God, nor is it like God;
it's a kind of fruit perhaps, but God is power.
This fruit is a sign of that power,
and all the beauty that one has made
points to eternities that escape
before the betrayal that gathers them.
God flees from every portrayal
that finds its own colors in the flow of time;
in all such paintings only the garment endures
with which the impatient ones illumined Him.

God darkens behind His worlds,
and the painter's hand alone errs.

Venerable Father, already wiser in years,
rebuke me in your anger if I speak out of vanity.
You've squandered God, but we are thrifty
with our God and place every act
that is done and everything that brings us joy
in cool boxes, smoothing every day that comes
like ironing a garment, and we secure all bounty
with the feeling that everything points to God
which passes unbetrayed through our hands.
We don't want to misuse God, in painting
and in prayer, merely to nourish our souls;
we only want to know that God stirs
quietly in everything we consider worthy.
The ancient patriarchs sensed God in some things,
but we want to know Him in many,
because we trust things more fervently
and are closer to them than the figures
of the pious fathers and holy women were.
Venerable Father with white hair,
every people has its own duty and purpose.
And if we were to gather around a *single* flag,
then ours would be a truly wondrous one:
we must honor our God as dawning among us.
Indeed, we've done this for centuries already.
Consider how in earliest Christendom we
practically wanted to betray God in honoring Him;
then the golden tribe descended upon us
like a giant's hand, one that

darkly suppressed our brash love—
and all fate that bent us to our knees
since then bound us to keep silence.
We've never *fully* belonged to any particular age.
We always lingered somewhere in crowds
that were larger still. We sat
while many stood on their tiptoes
trying to gaze into what's coming next.
We always have a present time
to which we belong. Sometimes this was
hard for us, but we didn't want to flee from it
and remained standing until we seemed paralyzed.
We were never distinguished for our holiness and passions;
    the sheen of antiquity faded away among us,
but we endured like a house's beams
and rustled always from rumors . . .

Thus I beseech you, worthy Father: be for us
a tower of defiance and like a man fortified with walls,
may God grant you endurance
for a time and a time.
Never free
a painter from the pressures of his work;
he might cry out in ecstasy in a moment
of sudden beauty to the God
we revered for such a long time
in silence (and even in song).
And then it begins for us—the time.
Other people are so noisy,
all of them laughing across the land;
God has ventured to come to us,

and I sense how He gazes upon us,
keeping quiet at his boundary.
Thus all should be silent
in the houses and at the gates
lest He flee back into His forest
and be gone forever.

This is the fear I've spoken of to you
(my hands tremble as I write this),
not for *myself*, this fear, because I followed Him
wherever He might have disappeared—
But He came, hunted throughout the world,
and they've all blinded Him for a moment:
some of them called Him poor,
others squandered Him like princes—
but none beheld Him in silence.
From stones and brows He rose,
disappointed with sounds, into the darkness.
"Do you have a garment? . . ."
is what He asked us.
And we're practically the last ones,
and what if even *we* chased Him further away . . .

O, don't brood over
my horrified words. They might infect you
with the trembling fright
that quivers in my fevered finger.

I'm a man of small stature.
But I had to tell you all this
because it's so urgent.

I feel it's already
beginning among us,
this witnessing to God in a false way.
Be tough, be hard
in opposing the world and its illusions.
You must order us to give ourselves to things,
to give ourselves to the paintings in your house
so that we might honor God for a time—
even when you need your hands for a different use
and return from work and hurry,
even if dirtied,
so that you might fetch Him—
but no one should speak and sing of Him
from out of the unknown wind.
Whoever does this has stolen God from us,
thus I must curse him with my most ancient curse;
through all the pages of the Bible I'll search
for the wildest words,
damning him with the darkest utterance.

Forgive me, Father, you who dwell in the rumor
of sanctity as if among the clouds,
for having lost myself
in zeal and vanity.
I've measured
my words with my anger.
I've raised my horn
to sound a vengeful song.
Now, however, I beseech you for a word of peace.
I'm turning back to my daily life
if you'll allow me to depart with your blessing.

I'll place the things again in my love, one by one.
I'll lift a great bliss once more
from all that happens in little ways,
and shall stir again each of my members
for one single purpose;
I'll sense once more the stillness
that has betrayed nothing.
I'm without fear and yet entirely alone,
but in this way I'm filled with *one* spirit—
my day will be like a thousand days.

The least among monks, an apostle.

In the monastery of the Anargyren, on the Feast of St. Charitina; the 5th of October.

[64]

The monk sketched the shape of his morning prayer, which on this
particular day was full of mixed feelings. And it went like this:

Only as a child was I thus awakened,
so secure in my trust,
to look upon You again
after every fear and every night.
I know, whenever my thinking takes stock:
how deep, how long, how wide—
You are and are and are,
having trembled all about in time.

It seems as if I'm now at once
a child and a boy, a man and more,
and I've come to feel that this ring
enriches us only in its circling.

I thank You, You deep power
that always seems to work on me more quietly,
as if behind many walls;
now the workday became simple for me
like a holy face
to my dark hands.

On the 5ᵗʰ of October, written down in the exhaustion of evening,
having returned home after having been out among the people.

[65]

That I didn't exist a little while ago,
do You know this?—And You say: "No."
Then I feel that only if I don't hurry
can I never be lost.

I am surely more than a dream within a dream.
Only that which yearns for an edge
is like a day and a sound;
it presses itself unknown through Your hands
in its search to find great freedom,
then sadly they let it go.

Thus the dark remained for You alone,
and, growing within an empty clearing,
a history of the world raised itself up
from stones that were ever more blind.
Is there one left who builds with them?
Crowds always want other crowds,
and stones are as if let loose—

none is hewn by You.

*On the 5ᵗʰ of October, when the monk had to make his way through
another day, through streets filled with carriages and riders—the rich
and those who celebrate senselessly.*

[66]

On the evening of the 10th of October, the monk prayed in the forest
beyond which, in the depths, the reds of an autumn sunset passed.
Along the forest's edges one could see the beginnings of a pale, small
profile of a waxing moon.

The light sounds in the tops of Your tree,
and makes all things colorful for You and vain;
they find You only when the day dies away.
The evening, which brings a tenderness into the room,
lays a thousand hands upon a thousand peaks
and among them the stranger becomes faithful.

You want to hold the world no differently
than this, with this softest of caresses.
Out of their heavens You seize for Yourself the earth
and feel it there beneath the folds of Your robe.

You have such a quiet way of being.
Those who intone loud names for You
have forgotten how near to us You ever are.

From Your hands that raise themselves like mountains
Your mute power rises with darkened brow,
to give the law to our senses.

The 10th of October.

[67]

You willing One! Your grace came
always in the most ancient of gestures;
when someone clasps his hands together
so that they're gentle
and centered on a little bit of dark:
suddenly he feels You becoming within them,
and like turning into the wind
his face begins to sink
with shame.

Then he tries to lie on the stone floor
and then stood up again as he'd seen others do,
and hastens to rock You to sleep,
afraid he'd already betrayed Your waking.

For whoever feels You can't boast of You;
he's terrified, and fearing You flees,
because otherwise strangers would surely sense You:

For You're the miracle that happened in the desert
for those who'd passed through.

After making his way among the people, the monk returned with a great craving for solitude, finding his cell transformed with bright autumn light. And the day gave way to a misty evening, bereft of sun, with rain close at hand.

[68]

An hour before the edge of day,
and the land is ready for everything.
Whatever you yearn for, my soul, say it:

Be heath, and, heath, be wide.
Establish old, old burial mounds
near your final verge,
as the moon rises above the flat
and long-gone land.
Form yourself, you stillness. Form
the things; they're still in their childhood
and will be obedient to you.
Be heath, be heath, be heath,
and then perhaps the old one might come
whom I can barely distinguish from the night,
bringing his immense blindness
into my listening house.

I see him sitting and musing—
not beyond me;
for him, everything is within:
heaven and heath and house.
He'd lost only those songs
he'll never sing again;
from thousands of ears
the wandering wind drank them in.
And for all that, it seemed to me

that I'd saved every song for him
from deep within me.
He remains silent behind his trembling beard.
He strives to reclaim himself
from all the melodies . . .
There, I come to his knees,
and his songs flow
murmuring back into him.

On the 14th of October.

*In the old chronicles the monk had read about the venerable blind
singers, the Kobzars, who in ages past wandered among the cottages
as evening fell across the wide expanses of the Ukraine. But he sensed
that one ancient Kobzar still journeyed through the land, going to
every door marked by solitude, whose thresholds were overgrown and
quiet from disuse. And from those who lived behind these doors and
kept watch there he retrieved his many songs, and these sank beneath
his blindness as if into a well. The days are long gone now when these
songs had left him in order to go their way in the light and upon the
winds. All that resounds now is their echo.*

Afterword

I implore you . . . to be patient in the presence of what cannot be resolved in your heart, and try to cherish the questions themselves as if they were sealed rooms or books written in a foreign language you don't understand. Don't press for answers that can't be given to you, because you're not yet ready to live them. And our true work is to live everything. So for now, live the questions. Perhaps you'll live your way into the answers little by little and only after a long time, without even noticing what is happening. For it may well be that you carry within yourself, as a singularly sacred and pure expression of life, the capacity to create and form. Let yourself be shaped in this manner, accepting with trust whatever happens to you, even if it arises from your own will or from some inner need of yours. In this case, too, give yourself to it, and do not turn from it with disdain.

RAINER MARIA RILKE,
LETTERS TO A YOUNG POET (16 July 1903)[4]

RAINER MARIA RILKE was still a young poet when, in the fall of 1899, he completed this collection of poems. Born on December 4, 1875, in Prague, a city belonging to the old Austro-Hungarian Empire, he came of age as part of a German-speaking minority there during the decades witnessing the emergence of modern Germany. His childhood was difficult and traumatic. In a letter written later in his life he described it as "one single terrible damnation, out of which I was cast up merely as out of a sea that is stirred to its depths with destructive intent."[5] His early schooling—first at the Junior Military Academy in St. Pölten near Vienna, and later at the Senior Academy in Mährisch-Weisskirchen—removed him from the grip of his overbearing mother, Phia, though such schools were ill-suited to a boy like Rilke, who had a sensitive personality and early artistic interests.

Rilke eventually persuaded his parents to allow him to return home, completing his diploma under private tutors as he prepared for the university entrance examinations. He intermittently attended university lectures for several years in the fields of philosophy, art history, and literature, first in Prague and later in Munich, though he never completed a university degree. By 1896, Rilke abandoned his studies altogether, turning his full attention to a career as a writer. During the next several years he published a series of reviews of art, literature, and culture, together with several volumes of youthful poems, plays, and a collection of short stories. By the early 1900s Rilke had established himself as an independent writer of some renown, and by the time of his death on December 29, 1926, he had become one of the foremost poets of his age.

In his late twenties Rilke entered into correspondence with an aspiring young poet named Franz Kappus, a cadet at a military school in Vienna not unlike the one Rilke had attended. The chaplain at this school had served at St. Pölten during Rilke's years there, and even shared stories with Kappus about Rilke's life as a student. Young Mr. Kappus had come upon a copy of Rilke's *Mir zur Feier* (*To Celebrate Myself,* 1899) and felt emboldened to write to the author, by this time a well-published poet with a growing reputation. Kappus included copies of his own poems with his letters, asking Rilke to help him discern whether he had talent as a poet. He eventually published the ten letters Rilke sent to him between 1903 and 1908, entitling the collection *Letters to a Young Poet* (1929).

This slender volume has become the most widely read and beloved of Rilke's writings, exploring questions of love and sex, solitude and creativity, art and beauty. In these letters Rilke admonished his young counterpart to embrace the vocation of being "solitary" rather than seek a public reputation as a writer, and to keep on this path despite its difficulties and precisely because of the loneliness it demanded. As the poet puts it, "it is good to be alone, because loneliness is difficult, and the fact that something is difficult is one more reason to undertake it."[6] Rilke went on to suggest that poets write because they "must create," and encouraged Kappus to "descend into yourself and your aloneness" in order to find out not who he *was* but rather who he was *becoming*. According to Rilke, only through this journey into solitude does one find the way to "live artistically, in understanding as in creating."[7]

The poems collected here in *Prayers of a Young Poet*, written several years before the first of his letters to Mr. Kappus, sound this theme throughout. He initially referred to this collection simply as "die Gebete," or "the Prayers," a cycle of sixty-seven poems together with a lengthy letter in verse written in a burst of creativity from September 20 to October 14, 1899. All of these Rilke attributed to an anonymous Russian Orthodox monk. In this original form Rilke included short annotations that give the date of composition and briefly describe the circumstances in which the poems originated, often suggesting insights into poems or passages that would otherwise remain obscure.[8]

As prayers, the poems voice the search for the God whom Rilke addresses not by name but rather simply as "You," often associating God with darkness, with depths, and with desire. The monk stands as Rilke's alter ego, voicing his conviction that God is as "alone" as he is—and thus the writer is one "solitary" seeking the company of another:

> You, neighbor God, when I sometimes
> wake You with loud knocks in the long nights,
> I do so because I rarely hear You breathing
> and know You're alone in the vast hall. [6]

And, elsewhere, he goes further in claiming:

> You're the second in [our] solitude,
> the quiet center of [our] soliloquies. . . . [17]

Prayers of a Young Poet is the first English translation of these prayers in their original form. They voice Rilke's journey of coming to see "how everything that happens is always a new beginning, and could it not be [*God's*] beginning, since all beginnings are always, inherently, so beautiful?"[9] This is a startling claim, locating human experience as the realm of God's "becoming" and thus identifying the search for the divine as one of progressive self-discovery or what Rilke several times describes as "ripening."

The voice and style of these prayers would have been highly unconventional for an Orthodox monk, deviating as they do from the ordered bounds of the Church's formal liturgy and dogma. What they give voice to is Rilke's own longing for a direct experience of God, telling the tale of an expectant love "like [that of] a bride," as he puts it in the opening poem, who believes that "to each one comes the thing each wills." [1] These prayers remind us to "set up our lives in accordance with the principle that advises us to hew to difficult things [so that] which still strikes us as most alien will become our most cherished and most faithful possessions."

They also encourage us "to try to cherish the questions themselves as if they were sealed rooms or books written in a language you don't understand." Above all, these poems reflect the admonition Rilke offered to the young poet to "live the questions" so that we might "live [our] way into the answers little by little and only after a long time, without even noticing what is happening." But noticing, paying attention, is at the heart of the artistic life, as Rilke understands it, and constitutes the deep character of the spiritual life as well. Only through such attentiveness, and the patience it demands, do we come to grasp Rilke's insistence that "our true work is to live everything"—everything, but above all that which is difficult, unresolved, and even painful for us.[10]

Composition of "the Prayers"

Rilke began work on this cycle of poems four days after arriving in Berlin, in September 1899. He had journeyed there to visit Lou Andreas-Salomé and her husband Friedrich C. Andreas at their home in Schmargendorf. The three of them had spent several months together in Moscow and St. Petersburg during the late spring of that year, a stay that shapes every dimension of these prayers and was to have a lasting influence on Rilke's life as a writer.

When he completed the collection some three and a half weeks later, he copied the poems carefully into what he describes as "an old black book," and gave it as a gift to Lou. The unpublished volume remained with her for more than a year until Rilke wrote to ask her to return it, intending to use the prayers as the opening section for an expanded volume he hoped to publish. At the time, Rilke was living in Westerwede, a village near Worpswede where a prominent community of artists had gathered at the turn of the century. He was newly married to the sculptress Clara Westhoff, who was by then pregnant with their first child. When the book arrived back in his hands, he described his reception of it as a reunion with Lou. As he put it, these poems were so "interwoven with happiness, recognition, longing and gratitude, destruction and creation that it recreated the pregnant intensity of that other meeting that I recall," an apparent allusion to their romantic involvement during the several preceding years. He went on to say that

> the old prayers resounded again here in this gray cell. They sounded so unchanged. Once again I was the tower whose huge bells begin to toll, vibrating in the interior and trembling down to the foundation, reaching out beyond myself. Reaching to you. It was all so close to me, as if we stood face to face. . . . Oh how I long just once to feel the hand within me that throws the larks so high into the sky.[11]

With these poems again in his possession, Rilke completed two additional cycles: a second, titled "The Book on Pilgrimage," written in a single week in September 1901; and a third, "The Book on Poverty and Death," composed in April 1903. In only lightly edited form "the prayers" became the basis for the first section, which Rilke eventually named "The Book of Monastic Life," and together these three cycles of poems came to comprise the book he published as *The Book of Hours* (1905).[12] The volume became an almost immediate bestseller, at least for poetry, helping secure his reputation as a poet of widening prominence.[13]

This collection includes some of Rilke's best known and most loved poems.[14] Their attraction has much to do with the way they give voice to a spiritual quest, one expressing a sense of Nietzsche's theological audacity, which he had come to know through conversations with Lou. Many of the images contained in these prayers seem to rise from the depths of the poet's unconscious, including the importance he placed on solitude as a condition of creativity, the role he attributed to "things" as the locus of divine presence, the centrality of desire in shaping the experience of transcendence, the role played by darkness in the creative life, and so forth. Such themes became motifs in his later poems, as if "the prayers" were the opening movement of a larger symphonic performance that continued with *The New Poems* (1907) before reaching their finale with *The Duino Elegies* (1912–1922) and *The Sonnets to Orpheus* (1922).

The Poetry of Search

All of Rilke's writings belong to a style Dorothy Sayers called "the poetry of search,"[15] which appeals to readers who know themselves as seekers on a spiritual path. They invite us to recognize how we "carry within [ourselves], as a singularly sacred and pure expression of life, the capacity to create and form."[16] In their allure they give voice to what Rilke calls "the stillness between two notes / that don't easily harmonize," pointing to what is *becoming* within "the dark interval" that is our life. [20] They engage our sense of wonder and entice us toward the posture of vulnerability and receptivity that Rilke calls "the Open" (*das Offene*).

Rilke's poems draw us on account of this allurement. They point to the experience of beauty as that which "change[s] values that have grown heavy," [21] opening us to the presence of the sacred in all things and in "every place."[17] [52] They voice the poet's longing for a sense of "presence" that emerges within *us*, above all in the midst of the difficulties we face and because of the darkness and desire we experience as loss or absence from day to day. They embody Rilke's view of religion as "neither duty nor renunciation; it is not limitation, but in the perfect expanse of the universe it is a direction of the heart."[18]

These prayers reflect the poet's long attention to the outer world as the locus of the sacred. They resound with references to nature, particularly allusions to the forest, with its varied moods and its plethora of flora and fauna. Such images, suggesting traces of transcendence found in the concrete actualities of things and places, continue to speak where language falls silent. They gesture toward the spiritual margins of experience. They call us to attend closely to the ordinary things around us, exemplifying the poet's conviction, as expressed in one of the late *Sonnets to Orpheus,* that "what lingers / is what truly consecrates."[19]

Poems like these reach through metaphor to the edges of our knowing, touching what Rilke here describes as the "hem" of God's presence. As such, they gesture beyond themselves, particularly in passages—and one finds them frequently in these prayers—that seem confusing in their literal sense. They presume that our experience of the outer world carries an interior awareness of the divine. They disclose Rilke's anticipation that "everything we had struggled to learn and everything we had failed to understand will be transformed suddenly into magnificent sense."[20] They invite us to "seize the forming day," as the opening poem puts it, since "[n]othing was yet done before I beheld it." [1] This is the "capacity to create and form" Rilke would point to in his letter to Mr. Kappus, reflecting the root word *poiesis* from ancient Greek which simply means "to make."

The allure of such poems has much to do with this sense of expectation. It also arises from the intense musicality of their style, the lyricism by which Rilke's language often edges toward song. It is thus fitting that the final poem ends with the poet's recollection of the Kobzars, the blind singers of the Ukraine whose vocation it was to pass on the ancient songs from one generation to the next.[21] Theirs was a tradition that depended as much on music as on memory, for these bards resisted "the heavy words" of prose "that people use nowadays," as he put it in one of his *Stories of God*, "these heavy words that can't be sung."[22] Conveying in their very form a sense of this singing, these poems draw us into what Rilke saw as a vibrant if almost vanished tradition—as if they themselves were lingering treasures of this legacy.

With this description, Rilke positions these prayers as an utterance out of solitude and into a waiting silence. Indeed, the closing words in this volume, at the end of the annotation to the final poem, sound this plaintive note: "The days are long gone now when these songs had left [the last Kobzar] in order to go their way in the light and upon the winds. All that resounds now is their echo."[68] The prayers thus close with a sense of the voice releasing its song back into the silence from which it had arisen, a dramatic caesura that exemplifies Rilke's notion that "the way toward the true value of all works of art goes through solitude"—in this case, as a lonely search for some resonance beyond this disappearing echo.[23]

Finding God in Everything

"Poems are not, as people think, simply emotions (one has emotions early enough), they are experiences," Rilke suggests.[24] But what kind of experiences do they come from? More than a decade after composing these poems, Rilke described them as expressing the experience of "unbelief" (*Unglaube*), but added that "such unbelief did not arise from doubt but rather from not-knowing and from beginner's experience."[25] This conviction, echoing the central teaching of Zen Buddhism on "beginner's mind," shapes his poetry, early and late.[26] In each of the first three poems Rilke starkly concedes, "I don't know,"[27] a disclaimer that reflects his reluctance to move toward closure.[28] It is an "unknowing" that grounds his view of how we experience the sacred—in ourselves, in the "things" of the world, and in the one addressed as the "You" who is beyond names, the God of the ancient Hebrews, who declares "I am who I am" (Exodus 3:14). This claim clears the way for the poet, unexpectedly, to speak of this encounter with the divine through myriad metaphors from experience.[29] He suggests, in fact, that while "a *different* God" seems to appear to each of those living in solitude, eventually they ". . . recognize, close to tears, / that through their wide-open pondering, / through all their knowing and negating," it is but "*one God wanders like a wave.*"[34]

   Seeking God as Rilke here envisions frees us to desire what we do *not* understand and what we *cannot* yet grasp. It opens us to a depth of experience beyond the conventions of tradition and the learned habits of piety. He suggests that a sense of this God must "happen" within us in the ways we come to know ourselves as a "beginning" for God, and in the longing this instills within us. He voices this conviction when he declares:

   You see that I'm a seeker—

   one who wanders behind his hands
   keeping silence, like a shepherd; . . . [56]

Rilke goes on to describe the anonymous monk who is the writer of these prayers as one whose "yearning reaches up to [God's] chin," until he finds himself "stand[ing] before [God] like the greatest of angels." [28] Our most primal identity, the basis for our finding this "beginner's experience," comes by our reaching for what we cannot grasp. For Rilke this meant that everything in our experience is capable of revealing the sacred: "I find You in all the things / I'm at ease with and like a brother," [23] for there is a "wondrous play of powers / that passes obediently through things." [23] Ours is the work of opening our experience to this sacred presence in all "things,"—"in the least of things" as in "the large ones in their ripening" [23]—discerning every dimension of our lives as the verge of the divine.

The Poet's Sense of "the Open"

The activity of this monk, who signs the letter to his metropolitan simply as "the least among monks, an apostle," [63] lends a particular character to the poems. He is an icon painter —or, as the Orthodox put it, an icon "writer"—who had

> . . . watched for You for a long while
> as if lingering above wells and along walls.
> And if others were to come and find me sleeping:
> God, don't let go of me with Your hands,
> for I am night from Your night. [59]

This posture of watching expresses a long and patient waiting, the kind of attentiveness inherent in the work of prayer as with the making of art. It depends on a sense of solitude that the poet finds at the heart of experience, one he describes in this curious image as a "lingering above wells and along walls." It is symbolized by the "night," the metaphor Rilke often uses to describe the spiritual. It remains to his mind a proper condition for the spiritual life and the basis for a creative life. It goes without saying that this is a posture necessary for the poet's work.

Near the end of this cycle of prayers the monk confesses that he has decided to set aside the painter's palette and abandon his vocation as an icon painter, turning instead to pen and ink in order to write poems that "face" God:

> . . . I want to gaze upon You and describe You
> not with the base of red or face of gold but with ink
> from the bark of old apple trees. . . . [61][30]

This desire to "gaze" and "describe" marks the posture of Rilke's prayers throughout the collection. Earlier poems in the sequence had already pointed to the monk's ambivalence toward painting: at one point he acknowledges how dangerous it is to paint God "in our own pose," [4] how fraught with failure all such endeavors are: "Whenever I *paint* You, God, You scarcely notice." [18; see also 6] The monk knows that the same danger applies to the spontaneous style and open form of these prayers which depart from the strict traditions governing the set liturgical forms used in Orthodox monasteries.[31]

Ultimately, this yearning for freedom of expression and authenticity of experience drives Rilke's monk from painting to poetry. But even this is only an interlude between the initial solitude of creation and the larger solitude that comes when the language of prayer finally subsides. The monk's ultimate desire is to give over the songs he held within him to the one who "remains silent behind his trembling beard," an image that embodies the expansive silence held in the poet's final admonition: "Be heath, and, heath, be wide." [68]

The Lure of Russia

As is hinted by many of the themes already mentioned, *Prayers of a Young Poet* bears witness to the profound lure of Russian culture and art for Rilke. On his first trip to Russia, in 1899, he and his companions arrived in Moscow on Thursday of Holy Week, just in time for the Orthodox Easter, the high point of the church's liturgical observances. Against the warnings of Tolstoy, whom he and Lou had visited immediately upon arriving in the city, the two spent the vigil of Easter wandering the streets of the Kremlin among throngs of Russians who had gathered for the celebrations.[32]

Rilke was particularly moved by visits that week to the Kremlin's Church of the Dormition, considered the "mother church" of Muscovite Russia. One of the poems in this cycle describes it as a "sobor," or "great church," whose "wall"—a reference to the iconostasis, the front wall separating the altar, spatially and visually, from the place where the people gathered to worship—"disappears behind the icons" while a dominating mosaic of Christ above in the dome serves as a presence "binding the whole church as one." [57] While he understood little of the church's elaborate liturgies, what impressed him was the extravagant "sense" of this worship and the dimly lit and mysterious grandeur of these churches, their darkness penetrated by the icons' glowing radiance.

Although Rilke and his friends spent only a week in Moscow before traveling on to Lou's home in St. Petersburg, the impression of this Easter was a spiritual awakening for Rilke.

He later recalled the thunderous impression of the great bells on the night of the Easter vigil: "I have experienced Easter [in my life] but a single time: it was that long, unfamiliar, peculiar, and thrilling night when all the [Russian] people pressed upon us, and the great bell called by the name 'Iwan Welikij' pounded upon me in the darkness, blow upon blow. This was my Easter, and I believe it will suffice for the rest of my life."[33] In the days that followed, Rilke spent as much time as he could in Moscow's monasteries and churches, absorbing the physical space and spiritual atmosphere so decidedly different from what he had experienced in the churches of Catholic Europe.

After returning from his first trip to Russia, in the summer of 1899, Rilke expresses in his letters a consuming curiosity about this people's simple and unlettered traditions. He clearly idealized the peasants' unaffected religious piety and simple connection to the land,[34] and from this point on everything about Russia—or "the East," as he called it—seemed to call to him. As he puts it in one of the prayers, "You speak to me from such distant lands, / and my strength / looks up to the ridges of the eastern hills." [39]

In an enthusiastic essay on Russian art written several years later, he valorizes Russia as still belonging to "the first day, God's day, the day of creation."[35] Russia, for Rilke, came to represent a contrast to the "fever-paced developments" that had gripped the West; it offered what he saw as a simple life, still largely uncluttered by the noise of automated machines and the pressures of industrial production and commerce. He idolized what he viewed as the slower, deeper, and more resilient culture of the "broad land of the East,"[36] which had a primitive vibrancy lacking in "old Europe": "The sense of our life in the West," he insisted, "is a great squandering, while in the steppes of our neighbor [Russia] all powers seem to have saved themselves for some kind of beginning which has not yet occurred."[37]

In a letter dated May 7, 1899, written shortly after arriving in St. Petersburg, Rilke enthusiastically remarks that "I now hear only Russian hours speaking [to me], and they announce themselves clearly and with the voice of the bells." He goes on to suggest that the world—and, indeed, his own artistic work—were edging beyond the "second day" of creation: "For the first time, the sea and land are beginning to separate themselves within me."[38] In one prayer, he refers to the imminent turning of the century as a metaphor pointing to the newness and anticipation he senses as a writer: "One feels the radiance of a new page / on which everything could still come to be."[39] [8] Russia came to stand for Rilke as a culture close to the creative origins of God, the first "beginning" that had the power to shape all others.

The God Who Is Becoming

This sense of a coming light, of an anticipated radiance, enabled Rilke to embrace darkness as the cradle of artistic perception and creativity. Clarity belongs to the surfaces, while darkness opens us to the depths where creation is continually occurring. His claim that "God darkens in the depths" reveals his desire to loose God from the conscious realm of the intellect, to seek the divine not through concepts or doctrine but rather in the experiences communicated in "the deep," by means of images and metaphors. Rilke's God is the "darkness from which [we] come," [11] the one who is "dark and like a clump / of a hundred roots drinking silently" in the depths. [3]

Across the wide reach of these prayers, the poet explores this "becoming" of God through a wide array of metaphors, many of an unexpected and unorthodox character. Thus, for example, he addresses God as "the ancient tower," "the dawning one," "the softest law," a "great homesickness," the "forest from which we never emerged," the "song we sang in every silence," a "dark net within which these fleeing feelings were snared."

Who is this "God" whom the monk addresses in his seeking and wondering? Not the deity of traditional theological formulations or conventional religious teaching; not the great being described in the church's doctrinal tradition as omnipotent and unchanging. In pointing to Rilke's unconventional understanding of God, Babette Deutsch observes that

> the God whom [Rilke] celebrates is not the Creator of the universe, but seems rather the creation of mankind, and above all of that most intensely conscious part of mankind, the artists. He is present and to be revered in all that "truly lives," but he is not yet perfected; in a sense, he is also the future, the incomplete, the unachieved, the cathedral still in the building, the wine that has not yet ripened. Only by a more sensitive approach to life, and to things, which have a strange secret life of their own, as every artist feels, only by an effort to understand the death that every life carries within it like a seed, shall [we], tutored by the artists among [us], slowly realize this great unorthodox godhead.[40]

Rilke's God is one who is always becoming, the "dawning one from whom the morning rose." [4] As he suggests in a letter to Mr. Kappus, God is "the coming one who stands before us for an eternity, the future one, the inevitable fruit of a tree whose leaves we are."[41] He goes further in one of these poems to declare that God, the You of these prayers, is "the beginning . . . and I, Your servant, / am for You [i.e., God] a new start." [21] This God is the one who is not "yet cold, and it's not too late / to plunge into [His] forming depths / where life quietly reveals itself." [14] This is the God who grows into "the uncertainty / that lies within this shadow of [His} face, and "completes Himself" before us, the One who "darkens in the deep" beneath the thin veil of consciousness. [41, 52, 51]

We encounter this God in the ongoing experience of creation, in "ripening" and above all in the primal darkness that represents each new experience of beginning. "The dark of God"[42] is not sheer absence but is rather a gesture toward a presence we can "sense" but cannot know: "Don't let go of me with Your hands," he cries, "for I am night from Your night." [59] Darkness is the place of God's becoming, the heart of the divine and the source of spiritual fecundity. It is the occasion of creativity, both divine and human, and thus stands as the matrix of the artistic life:

> I love the dark hours of my being
> for they deepen my senses . . .
> From them I've come to know that I have room
> for a second life, timeless and wide. [5]

Darkness allows for the emergence of this "second life" in our experience; it is the place of every new beginning, according to Rilke. "The darkness seizes everything," he declares, provoking his startling claim that "I believe in nights." [11] His conviction that "dark hours" are a source of life, and that the "night" becomes the cradle of artistic and spiritual generativity, shapes these poems throughout. The night releases us to the unknown. Darkness frees us to experience the divine as the "coming one" who is within every image and name—and, at the same time, is beyond them all. Such hours reveal to us what Rilke views as a beauty that does not "drain it of its shadow."[43] They mark the human experience of discovering again and again that our lives, even in the deepest darkness, are always at a *beginning*, that *we are always becoming*. The "dark hours" open us to recognize that we have the capacity for "a second life, timeless and wide." [5] To awaken this sense of life's renewing is the purpose of art, and the occasion of creativity. It is also, of course, the very substance of the spiritual life, as Rilke understands it.

How to Read Rilke

Rilke's poems display what one of his interpreters describes as "an orator's theatrical power, while remaining as suited to a chamber and its music as a harpsichord: made of plucked tough sounds, yet as rapid and light and fragile as fountain water."[44] This mixed metaphor offers a perceptive insight into Rilke's verse, illustrating how complex and yet subtle his poetry is—and thus how demanding it is to read. In the original German these poems exert a seductive power, shaped by the allurements of rhythm and rhyme and the entrancing sound of their musicality. They seem to want to be spoken aloud so that they might make their way from the reading eye to the listening ear. One might even say that they *become* prayer in this movement much as poetry itself can be understood, with Paul Valéry, as "a prolonged hesitation between sound and sense."[45] Rilke's images do their work in this moment of hesitation, this space between sound and sense, coming to dwell in the depths of the reader's unconscious beneath the surfaces of thought. This is particularly the case in those places where a poem's diction seems obscure and difficult to comprehend.

Poems like these invite us to venture into the unfamiliar, often precisely because of the strangeness of their images and diction. Rilke voices this invitation in a poem written a few years after these prayers:

> Whoever you may be: in the evening, leave
> the shelter of your little room where you know everything;
> for your house stands at the edge of great distances—
> whoever you may be.[46]

He knows that this "unknown" comes to us only when we depart from the constricting boundaries of the familiar, entering an inner solitude that does not depend on place or time or circumstance. Bachelard refers to this sense as "intimate immensity," an immensity that is a dimension of our inner being—or becoming, as Rilke suggests. "It is attached to a sort of expansion of being that life curbs and caution arrests," Bachelard notes, "but which starts again when we are alone."[47] This observation beautifully names the spiritual allure of Rilke's poems. Such inner immensity is a discovery that belongs to the experience of solitude, one that is not to be found in a monastery, or at least not necessarily so. It cannot be measured by conventions of piety or the formal traditions of prayer. It is an experiential path by which we find ourselves lured into "the Open," to recall Rilke's image. It is a means of widening how we experience the intimacy or "heartfulness" (*Innigkeit*) of our lives, the creative expansiveness of what he calls "the deep" that is within us—that is, "intimate immensity."

Rilke sees this desire for intimacy as a kind of "presence," one conveyed most aptly in metaphors of darkness and emptiness. Only an attentiveness shaped in solitude enables us to relinquish the familiarity of our expectations and open ourselves to what we might yet become—that interior solitude in which Rilke discerns that "*everything is within*: / heaven and heath and house." [68]

These prayers reflect what Rilke understood as the *process* of the creative life, which is not a technique but rather a distinctive way of experiencing life moment by moment. As he announces in the opening poem,

> The hour bows down and stirs me
> with a clear and ringing stroke;
> my senses tremble. I feel that I can—
> and seize the forming day. [1]

An artistic life, for Rilke, reveals itself in the ways we yield to *each* present moment. It expresses itself as a search for wisdom through attending to what is real here and now—within us, around us, through us, and beyond us. A creative life opens itself to experiencing the expansiveness of this interiority, which Rilke finds in *everything*: in anguish and in delight; in light and in darkness; in life and in death. We discover it when we allow our judgments "their quiet and undisturbed way of evolving, which as with every sort of progress must arise from [our] inner depths and cannot be pressured or hurried in any way."[48] Reading Rilke invites us to discover that our way *in the world* is at the same time our way *in God*. This path is "so terribly long," according to Rilke, precisely because it opens within us in each hour and in every "thing" we experience.

In an advertisement he published late in his life, Rilke suggests how we are to read these particular poems:

The Book of Hours is not a collection from which a person might select a poem here or there as one might pick a flower. More than any other book of mine, this one is a song, one single poem in which no stanza should be taken from its place, much like the veins in a leaf or the voices of a choir.[49]

We read these poems properly when we experience them like a long, complex song in which the varied themes and counter-themes, motifs and melodies, come to be understood in relation to each other. The meaning of these prayers, in other words, finds its proper shape in the "sense" gained from this inner complexity, taken as a whole. That is, once we have heard the entire cycle as "one single poem," as Rilke suggests, individual poems with their diverse motifs and images begin to speak—or sing—to each other. As they linger in our memory we find the larger shape of the song interpreting individual poems.

Listening to music does not make us musicians, of course, just as reading poems will not make us poets. But these prayers invite us to discover that attending to a work of art enables us "almost [to] become an artist," as he puts it in one of the annotations, if we allow ourselves "to be shaped by [these] poems. . ." [21]

With the gestalt of this "single song" in mind, particular poems from the cycle begin to reveal their "way" in us, much as happens in the use of a traditional Book of Hours. For example, in the second poem, the monk perceives God neither through metaphysical abstractions nor in personal terms but rather as a physical object, a "thing": in this case, an "ancient tower" whom he has been "circling for thousands of years." [2] What are we to make of such an image? Historians of religion suggest that the tower metaphor is found in ancient traditions of totem worship, an axis mundi that is the anchoring center of reality. Phenomenologists interpret an image like this in terms of its broader resonance in embodied sensation, pointing to the sense of an upward-reaching thrust into the heavens as manifesting a longing for freedom. Psychologists of religion—or the Freudians among them—point to the tower as the representation of a phallus, a projection of the male body's desire for union.

All of these senses of this image are at play in the poem. But this suggests that the question facing us in such a case is not *what* the metaphor means but rather *how* it means, an approach that brings us to discern dimensions in our experience that lie beneath rationality in the depths of the unconscious. As Rilke puts it in one of these prayers:

> And suddenly I have so many senses,
> all in their different ways thirsting.
> I feel myself swelling and aching
> in a hundred places,
> above all in the depths of my heart. [24]

When we face the "here-ness" of our lives, our *Da-sein* "in the depths of [our] heart," we begin to realize that our finitude is immeasurable, and that a plenitude of "senses" inhabits us in ways we generally do not notice. Thus, a metaphor addressing God as "the ancient tower" does its work in the "intimate immensities" of our mind. It takes us, as all images do, to the place of "non-knowing," as Bachelard puts it, which is "not a form of ignorance but a difficult transcendence of knowledge."[50] Such a metaphor functions as a tool of "the deep," a window into the dreaming imagination; it is here that the poem manifests its transformative power to lure us into "the Open," to awaken us to the "intimate immensities" that are within and all about us.

This inner movement depends upon the tension between the concreteness of the image—the "ancient tower"—and the abstraction of its referent—"God." The *Spannungsfeld* or "field of tension" created in such a metaphor is replete with resonances, moving us far beyond what the limited capacities of theological concepts or ideas might accomplish. Rilke's approach to God through such an image, therefore, reminds us that he is not writing as a theologian. He is a poet, writing as what we might call a "theo*grapher*," drawing upon the concrete images of experience to gesture toward God, "the ancient tower."

This use of metaphor to voice the language of seeking occurs throughout these prayers. It invites us to wonder who we *are*, and more to the point, who we are *becoming*—and who *God* is becoming. The final poem returns to the posture announced in the opening with a bold invitation: "Whatever you yearn for, my soul, say it," and then offers a vivid metaphor to suggest what this might be like:

> Be heath, and, heath, be wide.
>
> . . . .
>
> Be heath, be heath, be heath . . . [68]

Rilke's strange admonition to "be" such a wide-open and expansive "place" (*Raum*) encourages us to broaden our seeing, to widen our field of vision. This is the artist's way. It is also the deepest nature of the spiritual life.

He knew such landscapes from the moors around Worpswede, his chosen home at this juncture of his life. This village was then and still is nestled in a vast and open landscape of peat fields where farmers worked to cut and dry blocks of peat for heating. The call to "be heath" suggests that this place is an *interior* state as well, an instance of Rilke's affirmation of "the Open" as an "intimate immensity" of our experience. It evokes the visual widening of our sensibilities, the intimate opening of our heart. The resonance of this metaphor suggests spaciousness, expansiveness, openness: we are to *become* such a landscape.

As the poem moves toward its concluding strophe, we meet an unexpected guest: a blind old singer, one of the celebrated Kobzars, mentioned above and described by Rilke in the closing annotation. This "old one," whom the poet "can barely distinguish from the night," is the one

> . . . sitting and musing—
> not beyond me;
> for him everything is within:
> heaven and heath and house. [68]

He is the one Rilke invites "home," so that he might bring "his immense blindness / into my listening house," another allusion to the sense of spaciousness and possibility—"the Open"—that arises in the dark within and beyond us.

This is a poignant poem with which Rilke closes the collection. It brings the cycle from the open-ended anticipation voiced in the first prayer—"I feel that I can— / and seize the forming day"—to a finale shaped by an invitation to *become* "the Open." Once again we find ourselves poised just before the dawning of a new day, that time when "the land is ready for everything." And yet Rilke goes further, inviting us to *become* the land, to "be heath, and heath, be wide," a landscape that offers an expansive and seemingly unending horizon.

In this final poem, therefore, Rilke invites us not simply to wonder "whose soul this might yet free," as in the initial prayer; rather, he finds himself preparing to receive a guest, the "old one" to whom we might bring the songs we hold "deep within."

It is as if the poet is here calling us to discover what songs we hold within *us*, what music *our* lives might yet bring forth. As the poem comes to a close, we find ourselves invited to imagine *our* way into the vast solitude of this heath, the "intimate immensity" that we hold within us, and wonder how it is that we might find *our* way into a more spacious way of being, into this heath, into "the Open."

———

I am glad to acknowledge my gratitude to those persons whose help and support made this a better book than it would otherwise have been. During my years as a graduate student in Tübingen, Peter and Renate Kemmler became trusted friends, and in weekly conversations over meals explored with me questions of culture and philosophy, theology and literature—and, often enough, our shared passion for Rilke. I am also indebted to Dr. Ernst Lettau, who during the late stages of my work on this volume went through Rilke's poems with me, together with my translations, often with the light and heat of vigorous discussion and a steady sense of irony Rilke would have understood. Dr. Josephine von Zitzewitz, then Lecturer in Russian at New College, Oxford, offered wise guidance in making sense of Rilke's cryptic allusions to Russian Orthodoxy in these poems, references that remain largely unexplored by Rilke interpreters. Dr. Stephanie Dowrick, author of *In the Company of Rilke* (New York, 2011), has been a trusted conversation partner over many years concerning Rilke's poetry as well as themes related to spirituality and the creative life; I am grateful to her for her generous use of early versions of these translations in her own published work.

Over the years, I have also had the good fortune to read these poems—both in Rilke's German and in my own translations—with other colleagues in the academy as well as friends and retreatants in the United States and in the United Kingdom, in Australia and in Germany. Rilke's work inspired my inaugural lectures in 2007, at the Kirchliche Hochschule in Wuppertal, and in 2014 in my current position at the University of Applied Sciences in Bochum. My spouse, Dr. Ute Molitor, has had a steady hand in this work over many years, going over lines, phrases, and whole poems with me in my hope to make sense of Rilke's alluring but often mysterious style—and to let the ambiguities and "non-sense" remain when this seemed to convey the author's aesthetic and spiritual intentions. One of the most difficult challenges facing every translator, as these guides reminded me again and again, is to find and hold onto the courage to convey anew what might be *elusive* in the original, and to recreate some sense of the *allusive* with its often implicit range of meanings. In the case of Rilke at least, this means finding ways to allow English readers to discover expressions as strange and even wild as one finds in his German. Who after all but Rilke could write, without sounding contrived or coy: "I was song, and God the rhyme / still rustles in my ear"? [51]

I have also been fortunate in having two editors who assisted me over the years from the moment of this book's beginnings to its eventual publication: Lil Copan, then of Paraclete Press, took an immediate interest in the project, stirring my ambition to finish it and steering it through the early going before turning it over to her colleague Jon Sweeney. Jon embraced it with an equal enthusiasm, and has guided my work on it ever since. Authors fortunate enough to have had such editors and friends know what it means to be accompanied by stewards of the word whose intelligence and skill are matched by a true generosity of heart—Rilke's "*Innigkeit.*" Finally, my friendship with Gotthard Fermor over the last decade has been a treasure of inestimable worth and shared joy in things poetic (and beyond), leading to our collaboration in the publication of a new German edition of these poems: *Das Stunden-Buch* (Gütersloher Verlagshaus, 2014), for which I wrote the Introduction. Since then, we have made frequent public appearances across Germany to "perform" these poems, together with composer and pianist Josef Marschall and the photographs of Klaus Diederich included in this volume. This experience has reminded me how powerful the spiritual allurement and aesthetic appeal of these poems remains for contemporary Germans, alongside their widening gravitational pull in the English-reading world.

The work of translation is an intellectual and spiritual endeavor as much as it is an art form, one calling for a sensitivity to the intuitions and feelings that live within the poetic habits of language. It requires that we cross both linguistic and cultural borders, a venture we never make alone and one that is rarely simple but inevitably enriching. I am grateful to have made these crossings with such generous and wise guides as these. Their presence throughout this journey has reminded me that translation, always an act of "transgression"—that is, a "stepping over" or "going across" from the Latin *transgredi*— is first and last a labor of love. As such, it is one that deepens our experience of life's beauty and widens our awareness of its essential mystery.

Endnotes

1 Rainer Maria Rilke, *Briefe an einen jungen Dichter* (Köln: Anaconda Verlag, 2009), 18–19 This translation and all others, unless noted, are my own; further references to this work are cited as *Briefe*. The recipient of these letters, a young poet named Franz Kappus, gathered them for publication three years after Rilke's death, in 1929; this slender volume ranks among the best known and most deeply cherished of Rilke's prose writings—and perhaps of his work as a whole.

2 For a deeper consideration of this claim, see the "Afterword" to this volume, p. 91.

3 In this first annotation, it is striking that Rilke uses a first-person pronoun; the "I" refers to the monk who stands as the presumed author of the poems. All later notes use third-person pronouns, as if written by a scribe who accompanied this monk. As such, these notes read as if they were brief journal entries. These annotations locate the poems in an immediate context, and are probably descriptions of the actual circumstances in which Rilke wrote these poems. They also lend the poems a feeling of the "hour" of their composition, strengthening the narrative sense Rilke was after by describing particular episodes in this monk's daily life. They occasionally clarify oblique references in the poems that would otherwise be puzzling to the point of indecipherable, as for example in the case of references to the Church of the Dormition (see [57]). Rilke eliminated these entries from the later, lightly revised version that he titled "The Book of a Monkish Life" and published as Part 1 of *The Book of Hours*.

4 Rilke, *Briefe*, 24–25.

5 *Letters of Rainer Maria Rilke (1910–1926)*, trans. Jane B. Greene and M. D. Herter Norton (New York: Norton, 1945), 235. Further references to this work are cited as *Letters*.

6 Rilke, *Briefe*, 46–47 (May 14, 1904).

7 Rilke, *Letters*, 40.

8 The first of these, for example, declares, "On the 20th of September in the evening after a lengthy rainstorm, when the sun suddenly

broke through the forest's dark canopy and through me." [1]
All subsequent entries shift to the third person, as if written by a
narrator who had observed the monk's life and work.

9   Rilke, *Letters*, 60.

10 *Briefe*, 24–25.

11 Cited in Lou Andreas-Salomé, *You Alone Are Real to Me: Remembering
Rainer Maria Rilke*, trans. Angela von der Lippe (Rochester, NY: BOA
Editions, 2003), 69. In his biography of Rilke, Freedman suggests
that "the monk's vows and his simple ways produce an aura tinged
by the erotic attraction of asceticism." See Ralph Freedman, *Life of a
Poet: Rainer Maria Rilke* (New York: Farrar, Straus, and Giroux, 1996),
104. At this time, Rilke found himself reconstituting his relationship
with Lou from lover to lifelong friend and mentor.

12 The revisions Rilke made to this opening section prior to publication
were not significant. He changed words and phrases in some of the
poems, and completely revised three of them—one of which he
divided into two separate poems. He also eliminated two poems
completely, as well as the "letter" to the Metropolitan, for the edition
that became *The Book of Hours*. Two important changes, however,
distinguish this original version from the later published one. First,
Rilke capitalized all the second-person pronouns referring to God,
whereas later he reverted these to lowercase—perhaps to accentuate
the ambivalence of the address, given his later suggestion in a letter
to Lou Andreas-Salomé that he had written them to *her*. Second, as
noted above, Rilke removed the explanatory notes included in the
original version. In a letter to his editor at Insel Verlag he expressed
his hope that the collection would be published with the title *The
Prayers*, but added that in its form it "recalls the *Livres d'heures*" of
the later Middle Ages. It was eventually published in 1905 as *Das
Stunden-Buch*, or *The Book of Hours*.

13 Rilke's publisher, the Insel Verlag, reprinted this volume five times
during Rilke's lifetime, printings that altogether yielded some sixty
thousand copies. See Rainer Maria Rilke, *Gedichte 1895–1910*, vol.
1, *Werke. Kommentierte Ausgabe in vier Bände*, ed. Manfred Engel und
Ulrich Fülleborn (Frankfurt a.M. and Leipzig: Insel Verlag, 1996),
723–4. All further citations from this edition are referred to as "KA,"
followed by volume number and page. The popularity of this volume
did much to establish Rilke's reputation as a major poet on the fin-
de-siècle European scene.

14 A small handful of poems from *The Book of Hours* first came to the attention of English readers of Rainer Maria Rilke in *Poems from the Book of Hours,* trans. Babette Deutsch (New York: New Directions, 1941). A significantly larger group found their way into Robert Bly's *Selected Poems of Rainer Maria Rilke* (New York: Harper and Row, 1981) and Stephen Mitchell's *Ahead of All Parting: The Selected Poetry and Prose of Rainer Maria Rilke* (New York: Modern Library, 1995). More recently, two versions of *The Book of Hours* in its final form have appeared: a complete version, translated by Annemarie S. Kidder, was published as *The Book of Hours: Prayers to a Lowly God* (Evanston, IL: Northwestern University Press, 2001) and a partial selection— artistically rendered but with many poems omitted and others inexplicably truncated—translated by Anita Barrows and Joanna Macy appeared as *Rilke's* Book of Hours: *Love Poems to God,* (New York: Riverhead Books, 2005).

15 Dorothy Sayers, *The Poetry of Search and the Poetry of Statement* (London: Victor Gollancz LTD, 1963).

16 Rilke, *Letters,* 46.

17 For a discussion of "the embodied mind" and how metaphor functions as a primal mode of embodied perception and generator of "world-experience," see George Lakoff and Mark Johnson, *Philosophy in the Flesh: The Embodied Mind and Its Challenge to Western Thought* (New York: Basic Books, 1999), especially 16–73. Rilke's attention to mundane experience becomes a matrix for "epiphanies" in our senses, which he suggests are not to be restricted to special or extraordinary things nor confined to "holy" moments. These open us to discern the divine in every "thing"—a word Rilke frequently uses in this collection—and in the incidental moments of our experience.

18 Rainer Maria Rilke, from a letter to Ilse Blumenthal-Weiss (December 28, 1921); cited in Ulrich Baer, ed., *The Poet's Guide to Life. The Wisdom of Rilke* (New York: Modern Library, 2005), 163. Hereafter cited as *The Wisdom of Rilke,* 163.

19 Rainer Maria Rilke, *Sonnets to Orpheus* I, 22.

20 See Rilke's letter to Ilse Erdmann (December 21, 1913); cited in Baer, *The Wisdom of Rilke,* 11.

21 See also Rilke's story, "How Old Timofei Died Singing," written in November 1899, a month after completing "the prayers"; in *Stories of God,* trans. Michael H. Kohn (Boston: Shambhala, 2003), 32–40.

22 Ibid., 33.

23 Rainer Maria Rilke, "The Florence Diary," in *Diaries of a Young Poet*, annotated and trans. Edward Snow and Michael Winkler (New York: W. W. Norton, 1997), 32. *Einsamkeit* is a complicated word to render in English; it is sometimes translated as "loneliness," which is not incorrect, though this word narrows the reach of the German word. "Aloneness" is a better alternative, but this, too, fails to carry the wider resonance and atmospheric sense conveyed by *Einsamkeit*. I sometimes render it as "solitude," though also using "aloneness" or "loneliness," depending on context and the meaning Rilke seems to be implying.

24 Rainer Maria Rilke, *The Notebooks of Malte Laurids Brigge*, trans. Stephen Mitchell (New York: Vintage, 1983), 19.

25 See his letter to Marlise Gerding (May 14, 1911), in KA 1, 729. In a late letter to Anita Forrer (January 19, 1920), Rilke returned to this subject, noting that "in life one cannot awaken often enough the sense of a beginning within oneself. There is so little external change needed for that since we actually transform the world from within our hearts. If the heart longs for nothing but to be new and unlimited, the world is instantly the same as on the day of its creation and infinite." Cited in Baer, *The Wisdom of Rilke*, 59.

26 This phrase was popularized through the practice and teachings of Shunryu Suzuki; see his *Zen Mind, Beginner's Mind*, ed. Trudy Dixon (New York: Weatherhill, 1970).

27 Bachelard comments here that "in poetry, non-knowing is a primal condition: if there exists a skill in the writing of poetry, it is in the minor task of associating images. But the entire life of the image is in its dazzling splendor, in the fact that an image is a transcending of all the premises of sensibility." *Poetics of Space*, xxxiii.

28 For a further discussion of this topic, see my essay, "At the Boundary of Imagination: Rainer Maria Rilke and the Poetics of Theological Negation," *Studies in Spirituality* 10 (2000): 33–50.

29 He expands on this point in a letter to Lou's close friend, Frieda von Bülow: "All the things [of this life] exist among us in order that they might become 'pictures' in some sense or another. And they are not diminished from this, because while they articulate us in ever clearer ways, our souls immerse themselves within them in just this measure." Rainer Maria Rilke, *Briefe und Tagebücher aus der Frühzeit 1899 bis 1902*, ed. Ruth Sieber-Rilke and Carl Sieber (Leipzig: Insel Verlag, 1931), 17. Further citations from this edition are noted as *Briefe 1899–1902*.

30 The colors Rilke alludes to here provide the key to interpreting this metaphor: an icon "writer," or painter, first applied a dark red undercoat to the board before painting the saint's face; this is contrasted with the dark ink for writing that was made from the bark of old apple trees.

31 This tension between tradition and innovation marks this monk's struggle with his vocation, as Rilke portrays it. Thus, in one instance the poet explains in an annotation that "the monk sang with a loud voice as evening fell such that all the brothers opened their hearts, and instead of chanting their evening prayers this great song passed among them like a king." [49] Yet he is also aware of the importance conveyed by tradition as noted in his mention of the "Stoglav style" in the letter to the metropolitan. [63] The Stoglav Council, *Stoglavyi Sobor*, or "Council of a Hundred Chapters," met in Moscow in 1555, a gathering of church authorities called to unify religious practice and strengthen the Russian Orthodox Church against internal heretical movements, among other things. This council asserted the authority of Andrei Rublev (d. 1428) and his school of icon painting as the classical model to be imitated.

32 On this point, see Andreas-Salomé, *You Alone Are Real to Me*, 37.

33 Letter to Lou Andreas-Salomé; in *Briefe aus den Jahren 1892 bis 1904*, ed. Ruth Sieber-Rilke and Carl Sieber (Leipzig: Insel Verlag, 1939), 430; hereafter cited as *Briefe 1892–1904*. Also cited in Andreas-Salomé, *You Alone Are Real To Me*, 37–38. See also Lev Kopeler, "Rilke and Russia," in *Rilke, The Alchemy of Alienation*, ed. by Frank Baron, Ernst Dick, Warren Maurer (Lawrence, KS: Regents Press of Kansas, 1980), 113–36.

34 Rilke was enthralled by "arch-slavophile" precepts, propagated by many leading Russian writers including Dostoevsky and the late Romantic poet Fyodor Tyutchev (Fedor Tiutchev). Tolstoy, in contrast, opposed this as sentimental and foolish, and warned Rilke against what he considered a mistakenly naive attitude. Rilke uses the word *Bauer* to speak of them—which I translate "peasant" rather than "farmer" to point to this allusion more clearly.

35 Rainer Maria Rilke, "Russische Kunst," in KA 1, 734.

36 See Rilke, *Sämtliche Werke* 10 (1955), 494.

37 Ibid. For a more detailed discussion of Rilke's relationship to Russia, see "Rilke und Russland," in KA 1, 732–35. Such expressions point, again, to Rilke's embrace of "slavophile" views; see above, n. 36. Russia represents a critical turning point in the poet's life,

and a contrast to Renaissance Italy with its light-filled paintings of plump, red-cheeked Madonnas, the unquenchable ambition of Michelangelo, and so forth; see no. 30. In one poem he voices this contrast through an extended metaphor of "God the tree":

> The branch from God the tree that reached across all Italy
> *has* already bloomed.
> It might have liked
> to hasten becoming heavy-laden with fruit,
> but grew weary at the height of its blossoming—
> and now will yield no more. [31]

38 See Rilke's letter to Hugo Salus, in Rilke, *Briefe 1892–1904*, 67.

39 The contrast to fin-de-siècle sentiments of doom and foreboding is pronounced here and elsewhere in Rilke's writings from this period.

40 Deutsch, "Preface," in *Poems from the Book of Hours*, 6. For further discussion of this, see "Mit Nietzsche auf der Suche nach Gott?" in KA I, 735–40. For a thoughtful discussion of this question see Sascha Löwenstein, *Rainer Maria Rilkes* Stunden-Buch. *Theologie und Ästhetik* (Berlin: Wissenschaftlicher Verlag Berlin, 2005), esp. 39–95.

41 Rilke, *Briefe*, 42 (December 23, 1903). Rilke often describes God in these poems with references, direct and implicit, to a tree; for example, see nos. 31, 34, 47, 66.

42 This phrase is found in a letter Rilke wrote to Ilse Jahr, dated February 22, 1923; see KA I, 730.

43 Stephanie Dowrick, *In the Company of Rilke. Why a 20th-century visionary poet speaks so eloquently to 21st-century readers* (New York and London: Jeremy P. Tarcher/Penguin Books, 2011), 215.

44 William Gass, *Reading Rilke: Reflections on the Problems of Translation* (New York: Alfred A. Knopf, 1999), 32.

45 Cited by Giorgio Agamben in his essay "The End of the Poem," in *The End of the Poem: Studies in Poetics*, trans. Daniel Heller-Roazen (Stanford: Stanford University Press, 1999), 109.

46 Rainer Maria Rilke, "Eingang," in *Das Buch der Bilder* I, 1 (*The Book of Images* I, 1).

47 Bachelard, *Poetics of Space*, 184.

48 Rilke, *Letters*, 40.

49 "Gesprächsnotiz," published in Paris, 1924; in Rilke, KA 1, 731–32.

50 Bachelard, *Poetics of Space*, xxxiii.

ABOUT PARACLETE PRESS

WHO WE ARE

Paraclete Press is a publisher of books, recordings, and DVDs on Christian spirituality. Our publishing represents a full expression of Christian belief and practice—from Catholic to Evangelical, from Protestant to Orthodox.

We are the publishing arm of the Community of Jesus, an ecumenical monastic community in the Benedictine tradition. As such, we are uniquely positioned in the marketplace without connection to a large corporation and with informal relationships to many branches and denominations of faith.

WHAT WE ARE DOING

PARACLETE PRESS BOOKS | Paraclete publishes books that show the richness and depth of what it means to be Christian. Although Benedictine spirituality is at the heart of all that we do, we publish books that reflect the Christian experience across many cultures, time periods, and houses of worship. We publish books that nourish the vibrant life of the church and its people.

We have several different series, including the best-selling Paraclete Essentials and Paraclete Giants series of classic texts in contemporary English; Voices from the Monastery—men and women monastics writing about living a spiritual life today; award-winning poetry; best-selling gift books for children on the occasions of baptism and first communion; and the Active Prayer Series that brings creativity and liveliness to any life of prayer.

MOUNT TABOR BOOKS | Paraclete's newest series, Mount Tabor Books, focuses on liturgical worship, art and art history, ecumenism, and the first millennium church, and was created in conjunction with the Mount Tabor Ecumenical Centre for Art and Spirituality in Barga, Italy.

PARACLETE RECORDINGS | From Gregorian chant to contemporary American choral works, our recordings celebrate the best of sacred choral music composed through the centuries that create a space for heaven and earth to intersect. Paraclete Recordings is the record label representing the internationally acclaimed choir Gloriæ Dei Cantores, praised for their "rapt and fathomless spiritual intensity" by *American Record Guide*; the Gloriæ Dei Cantores Schola, specializing in the study and performance of Gregorian chant; and the other instrumental artists of the Gloriæ Dei Artes Foundation.

Paraclete Press is also privileged to be the exclusive North American distributor of the recordings of the Monastic Choir of St. Peter's Abbey in Solesmes, France, long considered to be a leading authority on Gregorian chant.

PARACLETE VIDEO | Our DVDs offer spiritual help, healing, and biblical guidance for a broad range of life issues including grief and loss, marriage, forgiveness, facing death, bullying, addictions, Alzheimer's, and spiritual formation.

Learn more about us at our website:
www.paracletepress.com or phone us
toll-free at 1.800.451.5006

SCAN
TO
READ
MORE

You may also be interested in . . .

99 Psalms
Said
Translated by Mark S. Burrows

These are poems of praise and lament, of questioning and wondering. In the tradition of the Hebrew psalmist, they find their voice in exile, in this case one that is both existential and geographical.

ISBN 978-1-61261-294-2, $17.99, Paperback

Practicing Silence
New and Selected Verses
Bonnie Thurston

"The old desert monks insisted that staying in one's cell would teach you everything. Bonnie Thurston shares, in finely crafted language, what she has learned in these deeply contemplative poems welling up from her own solitude. It is sheer grace to receive the fruit of her own spiritual journey."
—Lawrence S. Cunningham, The University of Notre Dame

ISBN 978-1-61261-561-5, $19.99, Paperback

Eyes Have I That See
John Julian

From rough folk-verse to high-flown poesy, from a nine-line rhyme to a six-hundred-line epic, both the style and genre of the poetry in this volume cover a broad range of poetic possibility. This is the first volume of John Julian's poetry ever published, revealing an important new American poetic voice.

ISBN 978-1-61261-640-7, $18.00, Paperback

Available from most booksellers or through Paraclete Press:
www.paracletepress.com; 1-800-451-5006.
Try your local bookstore first.